CONTEMPORARY'S

Put English To Work

LEVEL 1

INTERACTION AND COMPETENCIES
FOR JOB SUCCESS

JANET PODNECKY

SERIES ADVISOR
CAROLE ETCHELLS CROSS

CB

CONTEMPORARY BOOKS

a division of NTC/CONTEMPORARY PUBLISHING GROUP
Lincolnwood, Illinois USA

Publisher: Steve VanThournout
Editorial Director: Cindy Krejcsi
Executive Editor: Mary Jane Maples
Editor: Michael O'Neill
Director, World Languages Publishing: Keith Fry
Art Director: Ophelia M. Chambliss
Cover and Interior Design: Mike Kelly
Production Manager: Margo Goia

Acknowledgments begin on page vi, which is to be considered
an extension of this copyright page.

ISBN: 0-8092-3359-2

Contents

About This Book v

Unit 1 Before Finding a Job 1
Giving personal information including phone number and address • Completing simplified information forms • Reading and writing letters of the alphabet and numbers 1–10 • Functions: Introductions; giving personal information; taking leave • Subject pronouns • Possessive pronouns • Simple yes–no questions and short answers with verb *be* • *Where are you from?*

Unit 2 Places in Town 13
Identifying places in the community • Reading simple maps • Reading and writing numbers 11–20 • Functions: Talking about location; asking for and giving simple directions; asking for clarification • *Be* with prepositions of place • Questions with *where* and *when*

Unit 3 Work and Family 25
Understanding job titles • Matching jobs and places of work • Completing a simple biographical information form with information about family members • Functions: Telling time; talking about jobs and family • *There is, there are* • Simple present statements and yes–no questions

Unit 4 Help Wanted Ads 37
Understanding job titles • Understanding times, dates, and places • Reading simplified help wanted ads • Using ordinal numbers • Acquiring and evaluating information • Functions: Telling time; reporting information; talking about job preferences • Negative statements in the simple present • Adverbs of frequency • Simple *or*-questions

Unit 5 Questions at an Interview 49
Asking and answering simple questions about a job • Understanding general job-related vocabulary • Stating one's current job on a simple form • Acquiring and evaluating information • Functions: Asking for clarification; expressing satisfaction or dissatisfaction • *This, that, these, those* • *Wh*-questions

Unit 6 Job Instructions 61
Following and clarifying simple job instructions • Asking for and stating location of materials and supplies • Reading simplified inventory lists and work orders • Organizing and maintaining information • Teaching others • Functions: Giving commands and instructions; giving directions for placement of objects • Plurals • Adjectives • Simple commands

Unit 7 Money, Prices, and Paychecks 73

Counting and using coins and paper money • Understanding prices and identifying basic food items • Finding basic information on a pay stub • Serving customers • Acquiring and evaluating information • Computation skills • Functions: Requests; expressing agreement and disagreement • Count and noncount nouns • Questions with *how much* and *how many*

Unit 8 Safety Signs and Warnings 85

Understanding workplace safety signs • Reporting an emergency • Identifying parts of the body • Completing a simplified accident report form • Acquiring and evaluating information • Functions: Warning; telling about an injury; discussing frequency • Present continuous • Urgent commands • Questions with *how often, how much,* and *how many*

Unit 9 Skills for the Job 97

Identifying skills needed for different jobs • Stating job skills in simple terms • Completing simple forms with information about work experience and dates • Acquiring and evaluating information • Understanding systems • Functions: Telling about skills and abilities; telling about past experience • Statements with *can* • Simple past of *be,* statements and yes–no questions

Unit 10 May I Take a Message? 109

Making an appointment over the phone • Taking and interpreting messages • Interpreting simple order forms with alphanumeric codes • Serving customers • Acquiring and evaluating information • Functions: Making informal requests; clarifying by repeating; reporting past events • Questions with *can* • Future with *going to* • Simple past of regular verbs

Picture Dictionary 121

About This Book

Put English to Work is a seven-level interactive workplace-literacy course for students of English as a second or foreign language. The series spans the entire range of levels usually taught in ESL/EFL programs—from the beginning-literacy level to the high-advanced level. A communicative, competency-based program, *Put English to Work* features an integrated syllabus focusing on workplace competencies, general English-language skills, communicative functions, form, and culture. The content of each text has been carefully planned to meet the curricular, instructional, and level requirements of California's state standards for adult ESL programs.

The format of *Put English to Work* is designed for maximum flexibility and ease of use. Teachers in a variety of programs—from vocational ESL and workplace ESL programs to general ESL programs with a school-to-work focus—will find this series ideal for their instructional needs. In addition, teachers who work with multilevel classes will find these texts useful with almost any combination of levels because of the cross-level coverage of a number of the most important workplace topics. *Put English to Work* consists of the following components:

- Seven student books, from Literacy Level to Level 6
- Seven teacher's guides, one for each level
- Seven audiocassettes, one for each level

Each student book contains a Picture Dictionary at the back—an additional resource offering teachers a variety of strategies for vocabulary building. The teacher's guides contain extension activities, sample lesson plans, and suggestions on adaptation of the materials to a number of different teaching styles and programs, from integration of grammar to using the materials in multilevel settings. The teacher's guides also contain the tapescripts for the audiocassettes, which are available separately.

The philosophy behind *Put English to Work*—spelled out in greater detail in the teacher's guides—is interactive and competency-based. The series places a strong emphasis on developing the four language skills—listening, speaking, reading, and writing—in conjunction with critical thinking, problem solving, and computation skills. An important feature is the incorporation of the SCANS competencies, developed by the Secretary's Commission on Achieving Necessary Skills in a project sponsored by the Department of Labor. In addition, the series focuses on a great number of the competencies within the Comprehensive Adult Student Assessment System (CASAS).

Skills are taught within an integrated framework that emphasizes meaningful and purposeful use of language in realistic contexts to develop communicative competence. Target language, structures, and functions are presented in contexts that are relevant to students' lives. Students need to learn strategies and skills to function in real-life situations—in particular, those related to job search and the workplace. Other situations and life-skill areas are covered as well, notably health, family, and community resources.

The cultural focus of *Put English to Work* not only presents aspects of U.S. culture that many students need to come to grips with, but also allows for a free exchange of ideas about values and situations that people from different cultures naturally view differently. In the process, students learn about the culture that informs the U.S. workplace while understanding that their own cultural perspectives are intrinsically valuable.

Level 1 of *Put English to Work* is geared toward learners at the low-beginning level. Level 1 presumes basic literacy skills, though the alphabet and numbers are taught at the beginning of the text. Teachers with classes of mixed literacy levels may wish to use Level 1 in conjunction with the Literacy Level text. Suggestions for use of the two levels are provided in the teacher's guides for these levels.

Level 1 focuses on the development of beginning-level language skills and integrates workplace topics and culture as the text progresses. Clarification skills are presented and practiced throughout the level. Vocabulary is represented by illustrations, including the opening illustration of each unit, the illustrations in the vocabulary section of each unit, and the Picture Dictionary at the end of the book.

The SCANS competencies targeted in Level 1 are the following:

Acquiring and evaluating information
Organizing and maintaining information
Teaching others
Serving customers
Understanding systems
and the Foundation Skills

Acknowledgments

The authors and publisher of *Put English to Work* would like to thank the consultants, reviewers, and fieldtesters who helped to make this series possible, including Gretchen Bitterlin, San Diego Community College, San Diego, CA; Ann de Cruz, Elgin Community College, Elgin, IL; Greta Grossman, New York Association for New Americans, New York, NY; Bet Messmer, Educational Options, Santa Clara, CA; Michael Roddy, Salinas Adult School, Salinas, CA; Federico Salas, North Harris Montgomery County Community College, Houston, TX; Terry Shearer, Houston Community College, Houston, TX.

Unit 1
BEFORE FINDING A JOB

Openers

Look at the picture. Point to these things:

an ad   a bulletin board   a counselor

Where is Enrique? What is he reading? What is he saying?

1 Listen and Think

Listen. Circle the answers.

1. What's his first name?

a. Enrique   **b.** Ramirez

2. What's his last name?

a. Enrique   **b.** Ramirez

3. What's his address?

a. 410 Elm Street   **b.** 310 Oak Street

4. Does he live in Los Angeles?

a. Yes   **b.** No

2 Talk to a Partner

Step 1. Practice the conversations with a partner.

A: Hello. My name's **Raul**. What's
    your name?
B: **Fatima**.
A: Nice to meet you, **Fatima**.
B: Nice to meet you, **Raul**.

A: What's your first name?
B: **David**.
A: What's your last name?
B: **Lehman**.
A: How do you spell that?
B: **L-E-H-M-A-N**.

Step 2. Practice the conversations again. Use your own information.

3 Read and Think

Step 1. Look at the picture. Mei Long needs a job. She's at the employment agency.

Step 2. Read the text.

Mei Long is at the employment agency. The
counselor asks, "What's your last name?" Mei
answers, "Long." The counselor asks, "How do you
spell that?" Mei answers, "L-O-N-G."

Mei completes a form. She writes her
address (203 Oak Street), her zip code
(90824), her telephone number
(678-8934), and her area code (213).

**Step 3. Look at the vocabulary on page 3.
Then read the text again.**

Vocabulary

The Alphabet

A a B b C c D d E e F f G g

H h I i J j K k L l M m N n O o

P p Q q R r S s T t U u

V v W w X x Y y Z z

Repeat the letters after your teacher. Then spell your first name and your last name.

Numbers

zero	0	four	4	eight	8	twenty	20
one	1	five	5	nine	9	twenty-five	25
two	2	six	6	ten	10		
three	3	seven	7	fourteen	14		

Repeat the numbers after your teacher.

Days of the Week

Monday   Tuesday   Wednesday   Thursday   Friday   Saturday   Sunday

Repeat the days of the week after your teacher.

Word Match

A. Match the words and numbers.

247-8694   Three Twenty-Five South Street

214 South Street   eight-seven-six-two-four-eight-six

520 South Street   two-four-seven-eight-six-nine-four

876-2486   Two Fourteen South Street

325 South Street   Five Twenty South Street

B. Match the words and numbers.

287-9034   zip code

89 South Street   telephone number

78902   address

4 Put It in Writing

Write the answers.

Example:

What's your first name? ___*Jorge.*_____

1. What's your first name? _____

2. What's your last name? _____

3. What's your address? _____

4. What's the name of your street? _____

5. What's the name of your school? _____

6. What's the name of your teacher? _____

5 Listen and Speak

Step 1.   Listen. Enrique is at the Employment Agency.

Counselor:	Where are you from, **Enrique**?
Enrique:	I'm from **Colombia**.
Counselor:	Where in **Colombia**?
Enrique:	**Bogota.**
Counselor:	One more question.
	What's your telephone number?
Enrique:	**547-3568.**

Step 2.   Practice the conversation with a partner.

"Where are you from?"
"I'm from San Francisco."

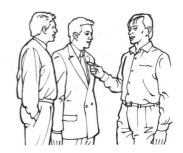

"Where are you from in China?"
"I'm from Beijing."

"We're from Ecuador."

"What's your telephone number?"
"773-8283."

Step 3.   Practice the conversation again. Use your own information.

6 Read and Write

Step 1.   Read the information on the form.

Name _Weber_   _Robert_   _Allen_
      Last   First   Middle

Address _108 Center St._   _10_
       Street   Apartment

Joliet   _Illinois_   _60880_
City   State   Zip Code

Step 2.   Write the answers to the questions.

1. What's his first name? _Robert._

2. What's his middle name? _____

3. What's his last name? _____

4. What's the name of his street? _____

5. What's his apartment number? _____

6. What's his zip code? _____

Step 3.   With a partner, compare answers.

Form and Function

1 I am from Peru. I'm a student.

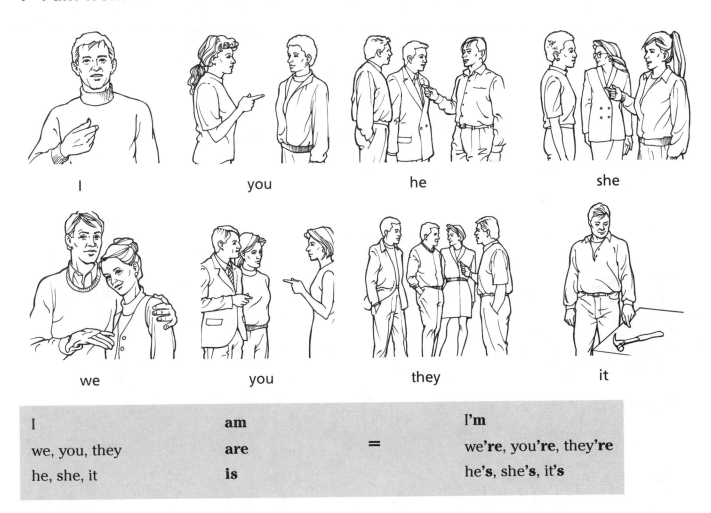

I	**am**		**I'm**
we, you, they	**are**	=	we**'re**, you**'re**, they**'re**
he, she, it	**is**		he**'s**, she**'s**, it**'s**

Examples

I**'m** a student. **I am** a student.
She's a teacher.
You are from China.
We're teachers.
They are counselors.
It's a hammer.

He's from New York. **He is** from New York.
She is a teacher.
You're from China.
We are teachers.
They're counselors.
It is a hammer.

Practice 1

A. Listen. Circle the correct words.

1. (he)   she

2. is   am

3. you're   we're

4. he's   she's

5. he's   it's

6. we're   they're

B. Fill in the blanks.

1. Jean <u>*is*</u> from New York. <u>*she*</u>'s our teacher.

2. Juan and Maria _____ students. _____ 're from Mexico.

3. Mr. Martinez _____ an employment counselor. _____ 's from San Juan.

4. We _____ from Vietnam. _____ 're students.

C. Tell a partner about yourself. Then tell about a classmate.

Example: I'm from Peru. Helena is from Poland.

2 My name's Raul. What's your name?

my	our
your	your
his	their
her	
its	

Examples

That's **his** computer.

That's **our** house.

A: **My** name is Raul. What's **your** name?
B: Fatima.

That's **her** car.

That's **their** cat.
Its name is Felix.

Practice 2

A. Listen. Circle the correct words. 🖭

1. (her)   our   3. her   your   5. our   your

2. his   its   4. your   their   6. his   her

B. Talk to a partner. Ask his/her name. Ask him/her to spell it.

Example: A: What's your name?   A: How do you spell that?

                B: Gina.   B: G-I-N-A.

3 Counselor: Where are you from? Mei: I'm from China.

Where **are you** from? I'm from China.   Where **is she** from?   She's from New York.

Practice 3

A. Listen. Circle the correct words.

Person		Country
Gina	👤	Italy
Hanh	👤	
Carlos	👤	Mexico
Kristina	👤	
François	👤	Haiti
Masha	👤	

1. are you   (are they)   3. is he   is it

2. is he   is she   4. are you   are they

B. Work with a partner. Ask questions. Complete the chart.

Student A: Look at this page.   **Student B: Look at page 10.**

B: Where is Gina from?
A: She's from Italy.

Student B: Ask questions. Complete the chart. Look at this page.

Student A: Look at page 9.

Person	Country
Gina	
Hanh	Vietnam
Carlos	
Kristina	Poland
François	
Masha	Russia

C. Complete the sentences. Use the chart.

1. Gina _____*is*_____ from _____*Italy*_____. She's Italian.

2. _____ is from Poland. She is Polish.

3. Carlos _____ from _____. _____ is Mexican.

4. Hanh _____ from _____. _____ is Vietnamese.

5. _____ is from Russia. She _____ Russian.

6. François _____ from _____. _____ is Haitian.

D. Talk to three classmates. Where are they from? Write the answers.

Example: *Enrique is from Colombia.*

1. _____

2. _____

3. _____

Putting It to Work

1 Pair Work

Step 1. Listen. Complete the form.

Name _____
        Last   First

Address _____
      Number   Street   Apartment

_____
   City   State   Zip Code

Step 2. Talk to a partner. Read his or her form. Compare your answers.

2 Pair Work

Step 1. Listen. Then practice the conversation with a partner. Use your own information.

A: What's your name?
B: My name is **Carlos Ibarra**.
A: How do you spell your first name?
B: **C-A-R-L-O-S**.
A: How do you spell your last name?
B: **I-B-A-R-R-A**.

A: Where are you from, **Carlos**?
B: I'm from **Guatemala.**
A: Are you a resident
   of **California?**
B: Yes, I am.

Step 2. Complete the form with your partner's answers.

Name _____
      Last   First

_____
Native country

_____
State of residence

Step 3. Read your partner's form. Correct it.

3 Group/Class Work

Step 1. Talk to two classmates. Ask each person:

- his/her first name
- his/her last name
- the spelling of his/her name
- his/her address and zip code

Example:

A: What's your first name?
B: **Maria.**
A: How do you spell that?
B: **M-A-R-I-A.**
A: What's your last name?
B: **Hernandez.**

A: How do you spell that?
B: **H-E-R-N-A-N-D-E-Z.**
A: What's your address?
B: **201 Oak Street.**
A: What's your zip code?
B: **60854.**

Step 2. Complete the form.

1 Name _____	
Last First	
Address _____	
Number Street Apartment	
2 Name _____	
Last First	
Address _____	
Number Street Apartment	

Step 3. Tell the class your information.

4 Culture Work

Look at the pictures.

"Hello!"

"Good-bye!"

Unit 2
PLACES IN TOWN

Openers

Look at the picture. Point to these places:

a bank   a bus stop   a store   a street

Where are they? What is Mei Long holding? What are they saying?

1 Listen and Think

Listen to the conversation. Then check Yes or No.

		Yes	No
1.	Is Mei Long going to the bank?	_____	✓
2.	Is the post office next to the school?	_____	_____
3.	Is it on Main Street?	_____	_____
4.	Do you turn left?	_____	_____

2 Talk to a Partner

Step 1. Practice the conversations with a partner.

> A: Excuse me. Where's the **bank?**
> B: It's on Green Street.
> A: Where?
> B: It's on Green Street. It's next to the **library**.
>
> A: Can you help me? Is the **library** on Main Street?
> B: No, it isn't. It's on **Green Street**.
> A: Thank you.

Step 2. Practice the conversations again. Use the places in the picture and streets in your neighborhood.

3 Read and Think

Step 1. Look at the pictures.

Step 2. Read the text.

Mei Long is at the store now. She works at the store in the afternoon. In the evening, she goes to school. The school is on Center Street. It's across from the store.

Sometimes Mei works in the evening. She doesn't like that because then she cannot go to school. Mei works hard.

Step 3. Look at the vocabulary on page 15. Then read the text again.

Vocabulary

Places

hospital

drugstore

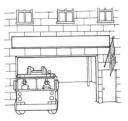

fire station

police station

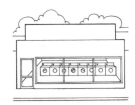

Laundromat

child-care center

Numbers

11	12	13	14	15
eleven	**twelve**	**thirteen**	**fourteen**	**fifteen**
16	17	18	19	20
sixteen	**seventeen**	**eighteen**	**nineteen**	**twenty**

Read the numbers after your teacher.

Times of the Day

in the morning

in the afternoon

in the evening

Word Match

Circle the place names. Then match the signs to the pictures.

1. First State National Bank
82 Main Street

2. Bridgetown Post Office
14 Oak Street

3. Newton Community Hospital

4. ABC Child-Care Center
17 West Street

5. Corner Drugstore

4 Put It in Writing

Look at the map. Complete the conversations.

School	Fire Department	Store	Laundromat	Bank	Post Office

1. Excuse me. Where's the post office?

   It's next to the _____*bank*_____.

2. Where's the school?

   It's next to the _____.

3. Where's the fire station?

   It's next to the _____.

4. Where's the Laundromat?

   It's next to the _____.

5 Listen and Speak

Step 1. Listen.

A: Where's the **drugstore**?
B: It's on **First Avenue**.
A: Is it **next to the bank**?
B: **No, it isn't. It's next to the school.**

A: Can you help me? Where's **the hospital**?
B: It's on **Park Street**.
A: How do I get there?
B: **Turn right at the corner. It's on the left.**

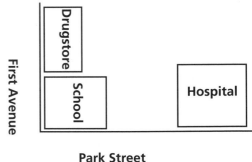

Step 2. Practice the conversations with a partner.

Step 3. Change partners. Practice the conversations again. Use the information on the map.

6 Read and Write

Step 1. Read the information.

```
CLASSES FOR ADULTS
at
SOUTHSIDE PUBLIC LIBRARY
18 Pine Street

ESL and ABE: morning and evening classes

Directions: From First Avenue, turn left on Park Street.
Then turn right on Pine Street.
The library is on the right, next to the school.

Call 427-1125 for more information.
```

Step 2. Write the answers to the questions.

1. Where are the classes? _At the library._____

2. What is the address? _____

3. When are the classes? _____

4. What's the phone number? _____

5. What is next to the library? _____

Step 3. With a partner, compare answers.

Form and Function

1 The post office is on Green Street, next to the bank.

on

next to

across from

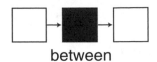
between

Examples

The bank is **on** Main Street.
The bank is **on** the corner.
The bank is **on** the right.

The bank is **next to** the school.
The bank is **across from** the store.
The school is **between** the bank and the drugstore.

Practice 1

A. Listen. Circle the correct words.

1. on   (next to)
2. between   across from
3. on   between

4. across from   next to
5. between   on
6. next to   across from

B. Look at the map. Then fill in the blanks.

| Fire Department | Store | Post Office | Laundromat | Bank |

Main Street

| School |

1. The post office is _____ Main Street.

2. It's _____ the Laundromat.

3. The post office is _____ the school.

4. The post office is _____ the store and the Laundromat.

C. Tell a partner about another place on the map.

2 A: Is it on Green Street? B: No, it isn't.

I'm . . .	**Am I** . . .?	Yes, **I am.**	No, **I'm not.**
You're . . .	**Are you** . . .?	Yes, **you are.**	No, **you aren't.**
He's . . .	**Is he** . . .?	Yes, **he is.**	No, **he isn't.**
She's (at school).	**Is she** (at school)?	Yes, **she is.**	No, **she isn't.**
It's . . .	**Is it** . . .?	Yes, **it is.**	No, **it isn't.**
We're . . .	**Are we** . . .?	Yes, **we are.**	No, **we aren't.**
They're . . .	**Are they** . . .?	Yes, **they are.**	No, **they aren't.**

Examples

Is it on the left?
Are they at the bank?
Is Mei in Apartment 15?

No, **it isn't. It's** on the right.
No, **they aren't. They're** at the store.
No, **she isn't. She's** in Apartment 14.

Practice 2

A. Listen. Circle "?" if you hear a question. Circle "." if you hear a sentence.

1. ⊙   ?   3. .   ?   5. .   ?

2. .   ?   4. .   ?   6. .   ?

B. Fill in the blanks.

1. Is the bank next to the post office?   No, _it isn't_.

2. Are they in Apartment 19?   Yes, _____ _____.

3. _____ the bank on Main Street?   Yes, it is.

4. _____ Jorge and Mei at the library?   No, they _____.

5. _____ Mei from China?   Yes, she is.

6. Is the school across from the bank?   No, _____ _____.

3 A: Where is the bank? B: It's next to the store.

Where . . . ?	**What** . . .?	**When** . . .?
places	things	time

Examples

Where is the bank? It's on Green Street. **When** is the bank open? It's open in the morning.
What is next to the bank? It's the store.

Practice 3

A. Listen. Circle the correct words.

1. (Where)	When	4. What	Where
2. When	What	5. Where	When
3. When	Where	6. What	When

B. Listen. Write the numbers on the mailbox.

1. Mei Long	Apt. _14_	5. Petr Talin	Apt._____
2. Tran Hong	Apt._____	6. Enrique Sabares	Apt._____
3. Jorge Ortiz	Apt._____	7. Jana Holas	Apt._____
4. Fatima Toma	Apt._____	8. Carlos Estes	Apt._____

C. Match the questions and the answers.

1. Where is the school?   It's the post office.

2. When is it open?   It's open in the morning.

3. What is that?   The bank is next to the store.

4. What is next to the store?   It's next to the library.

D. Work with a partner. Complete the chart. Ask your partner questions.

Student A: Look at this page.
Student B: Look at page 22.

Example: B: Where is **the bank?**
              A: It's **next to the library**.
              B: When is it open?
              A: It's open **morning and afternoon**.

Place	Where is . . . ?	When is . . . open?
the bank	next to the library	morning and afternoon
post office		
police station	next to the post office	all day
library		

Work with a partner. Complete the chart. Ask your partner questions.
Student B: Look at this page. Student A: Look at page 21.

Example: A: Where is the **post office**?
B: It's **across from the store**.
A: When is it open?
B: It's open **morning and afternoon**.

Place	Where is . . . ?	When is . . . open?
the bank		
post office	across from the store	morning and afternoon
police station		
library	between the bank and the fire station	afternoon and evening

Compare your charts.

E. Complete the sentences below.

1. When is the _____*bank*_____ open? It's _____*open*_____ morning and afternoon.

2. _____ is the bank? It's _____ the library.

3. When is the _____ open? It's _____ all day.

4. _____ is the post office? It's _____ the store.

5. When is the _____ open? It's _____ all day.

6. _____ is the police station? It's _____ the post office.

7. When is the _____ open? It's _____ afternoon and evening.

8. _____ is the library? It's _____ the bank and the fire station.

1 Pair Work

Step 1. Listen. Fill in the missing place names on the map.

| post office | hospital | drugstore | store |
| school | bank | police station | child-care center |

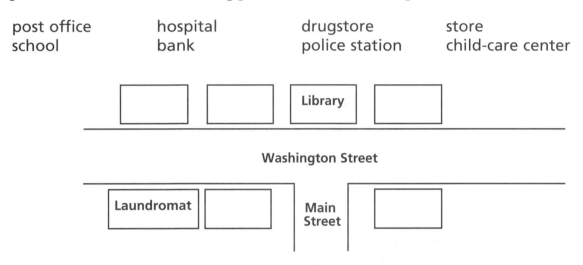

Step 2. Talk to a partner. Read his or her map. Compare your answers.

2 Pair Work

Step 1. Listen to the conversation.

Example: A: Where is **the library**?
B: It's **next to the school**.
A: Is it **on Main Street**?
B: **Yes, it is.**

Step 2. Ask a partner about the places.

Student A: Write them on the map.

| police station | school | bank | store | hospital |

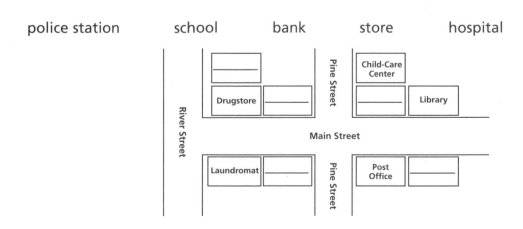

Ask about the places.
Student B: Find the places and write them on the map.

drugstore   Laundromat   library   child-care center   post office

```
                    Hospital                      School  _____
River Street        _____   Bank    Pine
                                         Street
                         Main Street
                    _____   Store   Pine    _____   Police
                                         Street                Station
```

3 Group/Class Work

Work with some classmates. Look in your neighborhood, in phone books, or in newspapers. Find some of these places.

	Name	Where (Address)
1. Store		
2. Hospital		
3. Library		
4. Post office		
5. _____		
6. _____		

4 Culture Work

Look at the pictures. People can learn about places by looking in the Yellow Pages, reading signs and newspapers, or talking to friends. How do people learn about places in your native country?

Unit 3
WORK AND FAMILY

Openers

Look at the picture. Point to these things and people:

a photo	a cook	a father	a brother
a nurse	a family	a mother	a sister

Where are they? What is Anton holding? What are they talking about?

1 Listen and Think

Listen to the conversation. Then check Yes or No.

		Yes	No
1.	Is Anton talking about his family?	✓	_____
2.	Is Isabel his sister?	_____	_____
3.	Is his brother a cook?	_____	_____
4.	Is his sister a teacher?	_____	_____

2 Talk to a Partner

Step 1. Practice the conversations with a partner.

A: Is this your **mother?**
B: Yes, it is. **She's a nurse.**
A: Does she work in the **hospital?**
B: Yes, **she** does.

A: Who's this?
B: This is my **father.**
A: What does **he** do?
B: **He's** a **cook.**

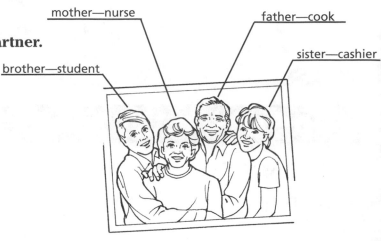

mother—nurse
father—cook
sister—cashier
brother—student

Step 2. Practice again. Talk about the people in the picture.

3 Read and Think

Step 1. Look at the pictures. Isabel Gomez is very busy.

Step 2. Read the text.

Isabel Gomez is a housekeeper. She works in a hotel from 8:00 in the morning to 4:00 in the afternoon. After work, Isabel goes home. Her son and daughter usually do their homework after school.

Isabel's mother lives with the family. She cooks dinner and helps the children. Isabel's husband comes home at 7:00.

Step 3. Look at the vocabulary on page 27. Then read the text again.

Vocabulary

Jobs

bus driver

cashier

mechanic

Family

husband   wife
parents

daughter   son
children

Time

one o'clock

two o'clock

three o'clock

four o'clock

five o'clock

six o'clock

seven o'clock

eight o'clock

nine o'clock

ten o'clock

eleven o'clock

twelve o'clock
(noon/midnight)

Word Match

A. Match the jobs to the workplaces.

1. nurse   **a.** school

2. cashier   **b.** hospital

3. teacher   **c.** restaurant

4. housekeeper   **d.** hotel

5. cook   **e.** store

B. Look at the clocks. Circle the correct time.

1.  six o'clock   (four o'clock)   twelve o'clock

2.  eleven o'clock   one o'clock   seven o'clock

3.  ten o'clock   two o'clock   one o'clock

4 Put It in Writing

Who is in your family? Make a picture or bring in a photo. Then fill in the information.

	Name	Job?	School?
Parents Father			
     Mother			
Children Son(s)			
     Daughter(s)			
     Husband			
     Wife			

5 Listen and Speak

Step 1. Listen.

 A: Is **Eva your daughter**?
 B: No, **she** isn't. **She's my sister.**
   She's a secretary.

 A: What's your **sister's** name?
 B: **Her** name is **Eva**.
 A: What does **she** do?
 B: **She's a secretary**.

Step 2. Practice the conversations
   with a partner.

Step 3. Change partners. Practice the
   conversations again. Use the information
   in the picture.

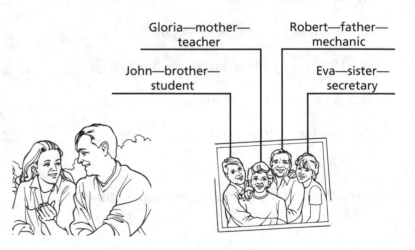

Gloria—mother—teacher
Robert—father—mechanic
John—brother—student
Eva—sister—secretary

6 Read and Write

Step 1. Read the information.

<table>
<tr><td colspan="3" align="center">Biographical Information Form</td></tr>
<tr><td colspan="2">Name Isabel Gomez</td><td>Occupation housekeeper</td></tr>
<tr><td colspan="3">Address 421 West Street</td></tr>
<tr><td colspan="3">Norwell, MA 02061</td></tr>
<tr><td colspan="3">Family Members</td></tr>
<tr><td>Name</td><td>Relationship</td><td>Occupation</td></tr>
<tr><td>Luis Gomez</td><td>husband</td><td>mechanic</td></tr>
<tr><td>Anita Gomez</td><td>daughter</td><td>student</td></tr>
<tr><td>Felipe Gomez</td><td>son</td><td>student</td></tr>
<tr><td>Ines Martinez</td><td>mother</td><td>retired</td></tr>
</table>

Step 2. Write the answers to the questions.

1. What does Isabel do? _She's a housekeeper._

2. What is her husband's name? _____

3. How many children are in the family? _____

4. Who is Ines Martinez? _____

5. Who goes to school? _____

Step 3. With a partner, compare answers.

Form and Function

1 There is one brother. There are two children.

There is a book.	**There isn't** a book.	**Is there** a book?
There's a book.		
There are two children.	**There aren't** two children.	**Are there** two children?

Examples

There's a hotel on Green Street.
Is there a park near the school?

Are there any children in your family?
There are three children in our family.

Practice 1

A. Listen. Circle the correct words.

1. (There is . . .) There are . . . 3. Is there . . . ? Are there . . . ? 5. There isn't . . . There aren't . . .

2. There isn't . . . There aren't . . . 4. There is . . . There are . . . 6. Is there . . . ? Are there . . . ?

B. Fill in the blanks.

1. There ___are___ six people in my family.   4. There _____ two sons in his family.

2. There _____ one daughter.   5. _____ there a library next to the school?

3. _____ there three people in the store?   6. There _____ some stores on Main Street.

2 Do you have any sisters? Yes, I have two sisters.

I have **some** sisters.
I **don't** have **any** brothers.
Do you have **any** sisters?

Examples

Do you have **any** books?
Are there **any** stores on Main Street?
Do we have **any** photos?

Yes, I have **some** books.
No, there aren't **any** stores.
Yes, we have **some**.

Practice 2

A. Listen. Circle the correct words.

1. some   (any)   3. some   any   5. some   any

2. some   any   4. some   any   6. some   any

B. Work with a partner. Ask questions. Complete the chart. Student A: Look at chart A. Ask about Suzette's family. Student B: Look at chart B. Ask about Han's family.

Chart A

Han's family		Suzette's family	
children	yes	children	_yes_
sons	yes	sons	
daughters	no	daughters	
brothers	no	brothers	

Example:
A: Are there any children in **Suzette's** family?
B: **Yes, there are some children in her family.**

Chart B

Han's family		Suzette's family	
children	_yes_	children	yes
sons		sons	no
daughters		daughters	yes
brothers		brothers	yes
sisters		sisters	no

Example:
B: Are there any children in **Han's** family?
A: **Yes, there are some children in her family.**

C. Complete the sentences. Use the chart.

1. Suzette doesn't have ___any___ sisters.

2. Han has _____ children.

3. He doesn't have _____ brothers.

4. She has _____ brothers.

5. He has _____ daughters.

D. Talk to three classmates. Ask about their families. Write the answers.

1. _____

2. _____

3. _____

3 He works in the office.

I **work** . . .	We **work** . . .	**Do** I **work** . . .?	**Do** we **work** . . .?
You **work** . . .	They **work** . . .	**Do** you **work** . . .?	**Do** they **work** . . .?
He **works** . . .	**Does** he **work** . . .?		
She **works** . . .	**Does** she **work** . . .?		
It **works** . . .	**Does** it **work** . . .?		

Examples

Do you **work** in the hospital?   Yes, I **do.**
Does she **work** in the restaurant?   Yes, she **does.**
Do they **work** in the store?   Yes, they **do.**

Practice 3

A. Listen. Circle the correct words.

1. (work)   works   3. work   works   5. work   works

2. work   works   4. work   works   6. work   works

B. Circle the correct form of verb.

1. Where do you ((work)/works)?   4. Yes, she (work/works) every day.

2. I (work/works) in the hotel.   5. We (work/works) in the morning.

3. Does Isabel (work/works) here?   6. Luis (work/works) in the afternoon.

C. Work with a partner. Student A: Look at this page. Student B: Look at page 34.
Ask your partner questions about the people. Fill in the missing information.

Example:
B: **When** does **Isabel** work?
A: **Isabel** works **in the morning and afternoon.**

Name	Where does . . . work?	When does . . . work?
Isabel	_____	morning, afternoon
Paul	store	_____
Anita	_____	morning
Ed	office	_____

Work with a partner. Student B: Look at this page. Student A: Look at page 33. Ask your partner questions about the people. Fill in the missing information.

Example:
A: **Where** does Isabel work?
B: Isabel works in a **hotel.**

Name	Where does . . . work?	When does . . . work?
Isabel	hotel	_____
Paul	_____	afternoon
Anita	school	_____
Ed	_____	afternoon, evening

D. Complete the sentences. Use the information in your charts.

1. When does Isabel work?

   She __*works*__ in the __*afternoon*__ and morning.

2. Where does Isabel work?

   She works in a _____.

3. When does Paul work?

   Paul works in the _____.

4. Where does Paul work?

   He _____ in a _____.

5. When does Anita work?

   She _____ in the _____.

6. Where does Anita work?

   She works in a _____.

7. When does Ed work?

   He works in the _____ and _____.

8. Where does Ed work?

   He works in an _____.

Putting It to Work

1 Pair Work

Step 1. Listen. With a partner, fill in the missing information on the form.

mother brother father husband wife teacher

son daughter student bus driver nurse child-care worker

Biographical Information Form		
Name ___*Bernard Santil*___	Occupation **1.**_____	
Family Members		
Name	Relationship	Occupation
Daphne Santil	**2.**	**3.**
Marie Santil	**4.**	**5.**
Pierre Santil	**6.**	**7.**

Step 2. Talk to another pair of classmates. Compare your answers.

2 Pair Work

Step 1. Listen to the conversation.

Step 2. Student A: Look at this page. Student B: Look at page 36. Ask about the people in the chart. Complete the chart with your partner's information. Fill in the jobs and times.

Example:
B: What does **Jana** do?
A: She's a **child-care worker.**
B: When does she work?
A: She works **from 10:00 to 4:00.**

Person	Job (What . . . ?)	Time (When . . . ?)
Jana (she)	child-care worker	10:00–4:00
Robert (he)		
Angela (she)	cashier	8:00–2:00
Kim (she)		
Fatima (she)	cook	2:00–10:00
Pierre (he)		

Student B: Look at this page. Student A: Look at page 35. Ask about the people in the chart. Complete the chart with your partner's information. Fill in the jobs and times.

Example:
A: What does **Robert** do?
B: **He's** a **bus driver.**
A: When does **he** work?
B: **He** works **from 10:00 to 7:00.**

Person	Job (What . . . ?)	Time (When. . .?)
Jana (she)		
Robert (he)	bus driver	10:00–7:00
Angela (she)		
Kim (she)	housekeeper	7:00–3:00
Fatima (she)		
Pierre (he)	secretary	9:00–1:00

3 Group/Class Work

Work with some classmates. Ask friends about their jobs and family members.

Name	What do you do?	Do you have a husband/wife?	Do you have any brothers/sisters?
1.			
2.			
3.			
4.			

4 Culture Work

Are these jobs for men or women? What do you think? Mark each job with a check mark under *Men*, *Women*, or *Men or Women*. Then talk about it with your class.

	Men	Women	Men or Women
Cook			
Nurse			
Teacher			
Mechanic			
Child-care worker			
Bus driver			
Secretary			

Unit 4
HELP WANTED ADS

Openers

Look at the picture. Point to these things and signs:

a want ad
Help Wanted

a newspaper
Employment

a bulletin board

Where are they? What are they looking at? What are they talking about?

1 Listen and Think

Listen to the conversation. Then check Yes or No.

	Yes	No
1. Does Mei Long like her job?	_____	✔
2. Is Anton looking for a new job?	_____	_____
3. Does Mei Long want to work in the afternoon?	_____	_____
4. Is the job in a bank?	_____	_____

2 Talk to a Partner

Step 1. Practice the conversations with a partner.

A: How's your job?
B: Not too good. I don't like it. I'm looking for a new job.
A: What do you want to do?
B: I want to be a **secretary**.

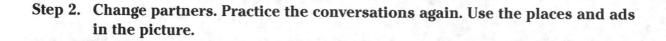

A: I'm looking for a job.
B: There are some want ads **on the bulletin board**.
A: Thanks.

Step 2. Change partners. Practice the conversations again. Use the places and ads in the picture.

3 Read and Think

Step 1. Look at the picture. Mei Long wants a new job.

Step 2. Read the text.

Mei Long is a cashier, but she doesn't like her job. She doesn't want to work in the afternoons and in the evenings. She's looking for another job.

There are two ads for cashiers on the employment bulletin board. The cashier at QuickShop works from 6:00 in the evening to 11:00 o'clock at night. The job at Foodland Supermarket is from 8:00 in the morning to 1:00 in the afternoon. Mei wants to ask about the job at Foodland.

Step 3. Read the text again. Some of the words are for things in the picture. Find them and circle them above.

Vocabulary

Jobs

welder

gardener

wait staff

janitor

painter

clerk

Months

January

February

March

April

May

June

July

August

September

October

November

December

Ordinal Numbers

1st first	9th ninth	17th seventeenth	25th twenty-fifth
2nd second	10th tenth	18th eighteenth	26th twenty-sixth
3rd third	11th eleventh	19th nineteenth	27th twenty-seventh
4th fourth	12th twelfth	20th twentieth	28th twenty-eighth
5th fifth	13th thirteenth	21st twenty-first	29th twenty-ninth
6th sixth	14th fourteenth	22nd twenty-second	30th thirtieth
7th seventh	15th fifteenth	23rd twenty-third	31st thirty-first
8th eighth	16th sixteenth	24th twenty-fourth	

Word Match

A. Listen. Circle the dates you hear.

1. (Oct. 4)	Aug. 4	Dec. 4	**5.** Jan. 25	June 25	July 25
2. Mar. 10	May 10	Nov. 10	**6.** Feb. 2	Feb. 22	Dec. 2
3. Apr. 16	Oct. 16	Apr. 26	**7.** Sept. 1	Feb. 1	Dec. 21
4. July 28	June 8	Aug. 8	**8.** Nov. 17	Mar. 17	Nov. 7

B. Listen. Write the dates you hear.

1. _March 30_

2. _____

3. _____

4. _____

5. _____

C. Match the people with the job titles. Write the numbers by the titles.

1.

2.

3.

4.

5.

6.

Gardener _____

Clerk _____

Welder _____

Janitor _____

Painter _____

Wait staff ___4___

4 Put It in Writing

Complete the sentences with the correct times and dates.

Example: *Today is Tuesday, December 6.*

1. Today is (day) _____ , (month and date) _____ .

2. Right now, it is (time) _____ .

3. Class starts at (time) _____ .

4. I arrive at class at (time) _____ .

5. My birthday is on (month and date) _____ .

6. Tomorrow is (day) _____ , (month and date) _____ .

7. Class ends at (time) _____ .

8. My next class is on (month and date) _____ .

9. My last class is on (month and date) _____ .

5 Listen and Speak

Step 1. Listen.

A: Is this job in the evening?
B: **Yes. It's from 3:00 to 11:00.**
A: What's the phone number?
B: **555-0025.**
A: **555-0025?**
B: Yes, that's right.

> Janitor Needed
> Hours: 3 P.M.–11 P.M.
> Clark School, 213 North St.
> 555-0025

A: I need a job in the morning.
B: Here's a job **from 8:00 to 12:00.**
A: Where is it?
B: It's at **118 Park Street.**
A: Did you say **118 Park Street** or **180 Park Street?**
B: **118 Park Street.**

> Gardener
> Hours: 8 A.M.–12 A.M
> Garden Care Center
> 118 Park Street
> 555-8242

Step 2. Practice the conversations with a partner.

Step 3. Change partners. Practice the conversations again. Use the information on the want ads.

6 Read and Write

Step 1. Read the information.

```
┌────────────────────────────────────────────────────────────────────────────┐
│                      Employment and Training                               │
│                                                                            │
│  Name  Albert           Laura              Anne                            │
│        Last             First              Middle                          │
│                                                                            │
│  Address  18 Central Street                                                │
│           Norwell, MA 02061                                                │
│                                                                            │
│  Phone Number  555-7334          Date of Birth  Apr. 4, 1976               │
│                                                                            │
│  Occupation  cashier             Date of Arrival  Dec. 12, 1992            │
│                                                                            │
│  Do you have a job now?    Yes  ✔    No ____                               │
│                                                                            │
│        Laura Albert                    Oct. 23, 1997                        │
│  Signature                      Date                                       │
└────────────────────────────────────────────────────────────────────────────┘
```

Step 2.   Write the answers to the questions.

1. What's her first name? _Laura_ _____

2. What's her last name? _____

3. What's her phone number? _____

4. What is her date of birth? _____

5. What's her occupation? _____

6. What was her date of arrival in the U.S.? _____

Step 3.   With a partner, compare answers.

Form and Function

1 I don't work in the morning.

I **work** . . .	I **don't work** . . .	**Do** I **work** . . .?
You **work** . . .	You **don't work** . . .	**Do** you **work** . . .?
He **works** . . .	He **doesn't work** . . .	**Does** he **work** . . .?
She **works** . . .	She **doesn't work** . . .	**Does** she **work** . . .?
We **work** . . .	We **don't work** . . .	**Do** we **work** . . .?
They **work** . . .	They **don't work** . . .	**Do** they **work** . . .?

Examples

I **like** my job.
She **calls** the employment office.
Do they **work** in the bank?
Does she **want** a new job?

I **don't like** my job.
She **doesn't call** the school.
No, they **don't**.
No, she **doesn't**.

Practice 1

A. Listen. Circle the correct words.

1. work (don't work)

2. likes doesn't like

3. play don't play

4. reads doesn't read

5. call don't call

6. walks doesn't walk

B. Look at the chart. Circle the correct forms of the verbs.

1. Al ((works)/doesn't work) in the morning.

2. Rita (works/doesn't work) in the morning.

3. Al (reads/doesn't read) in the afternoon.

4. Rita (studies/doesn't study) in the evening.

5. Al (plays/doesn't play) soccer in the afternoon.

6. Rita (reads/doesn't read) in the afternoon.

	in the morning	in the afternoon	in the evening
Al	works	plays	reads
Rita	reads	works	studies

2 I never watch TV.

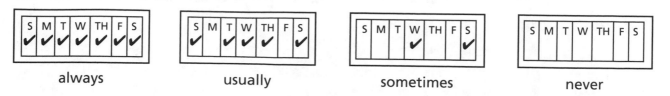

always	usually	sometimes	never

Examples

We **usually** watch TV at night.   I **never** read in the morning.
Tom **sometimes** works all day.   They **sometimes** visit in the afternoon.

Practice 2

A. Listen. Check the word you hear.

	always	usually	sometimes	never	
Flores		✔			cooks dinner
Bernard					walks
Daphne					reads
Marie					plays soccer
Pierre					studies

B. Check the words that describe your activities.

	always	usually	sometimes	never	
					cook dinner
					walk to work
					read
					play soccer
					study

C. Tell a classmate about your activities.

3 Do you want to be a cashier or a cook?

Is he a <u>painter</u> **or** a <u>gardener</u>?	He's a painter.
Does she work in <u>a school</u> **or** <u>an office</u>?	She works in an office.
Are you <u>happy</u> **or** <u>sad</u>?	I'm happy.
Is today May <u>8th</u> **or** <u>9th</u>?	Today is May 8th.

Examples

Do you want to be <u>a nurse</u> **or** <u>a teacher</u>?	I want to be a nurse.
Do you work <u>in the morning</u> **or** <u>in the evening</u>?	I work in the evening.

Practice 3

A. Listen. Circle the answer.

1. clerk   **(cashier)**
2. afternoon   evening
3. bank   library

4. Sept. 1   Sept. 21
5. 555-1234   555-4321
6. 8:00   10:00

B. Student A: Look at this page. Student B: Look at page 46. Ask a partner some "or" questions about the ads.

Role 1. Student A: Ask your partner questions about Ad A. Follow the model. Circle the answers.

Example:

A: Do you want the job as a
   waiter or the job as a **cook?**
B: I want the job as a **cook.**
A: Do you want **morning**
   hours or **evening** hours?
B: **Morning** hours.
A: OK. There's a good job in **a restaurant.** The phone number is **687-9754.**

A	B
Help Wanted	Help Wanted
Job Title: Clerk or Cashier	Job Title: Janitor
Hours: Morning or Evening	Hours: Morning
Place: Bank or Store	Place: School
Phone: 555-8212 or 555-2212	Phone: 555-8383

Role 2. Answer your partner's questions about Ad B. Answer with the information in Ad B.

Student B: Look at this page. Student A: Look at page 45. Ask a partner some "or" questions about the ads.

Role 1.   Student B: Answer your partner's questions about Ad A. Answer with the information in Ad A.

Example:

A: Do you want the job as a
   waiter or the job as a **cook?**
B: I want the job as a **cook.**
A: Do you want **morning** hours
   or **evening** hours?
B: **Morning** hours.

<table>
<tr><td align="center">A</td><td align="center">B</td></tr>
<tr><td>Help Wanted
Job Title: Cashier
Hours: Morning
Place: Store
Phone: 555-8212</td><td>Help Wanted
Job Title: Janitor or Painter
Hours: Morning or Afternoon
Place: Office or School
Phone: 555-3383 or 555-8383</td></tr>
</table>

Role 2. Student B: Ask your partner questions about Ad B. Circle the answers.

Compare your answers.

C.   Complete the sentences below.

1. Does Mario want _an office job_

   or a restaurant job ?

an office job   a restaurant job

2. He wants _____

   _____ .

3. Does Jean want _____

   _____ ?

a day job   a night job

4. She wants _____

   _____ .

D.   Work with a partner. Ask your partner the same questions.

Putting It to Work

1 Pair Work

Step 1.   Listen. Write the names of the people under the ads you think they'd like.

Carlos	Martina	Sokhom	George

Gardener Wanted Hrs. 7 A.M.–12 P.M.	Wait staff Hrs. 4 P.M.–9 P.M.	Child-care workers Hrs. 8 A.M.–12 P.M.	Clerk Hrs. 1 P.M.–9 P.M.
_____	_____	_____	_____

Step 2.   Talk to a partner. Compare your answers.

2 Pair Work

Step 1.   Listen to the conversation.

Example: A: What are the hours for the
                clerk?
            B: From 10:00 in the morning to
                2:00 in the afternoon.

A: Where is the job?
B: It's at the bank.
A: What's the phone number?
B: It's 555-3233.

Step 2.   Ask about the jobs below.

Student A

A	B	C	D
Clerk Wanted Hrs. 10 A.M.–2 P.M. State Bank Call: 555-3233	Welders Hrs. _____ Taylor Iron Works Call: _____	Painter Hrs. 9–5 _____ Call: 555-9076	Cashiers Hrs. _____ Hillside Pharmacy Call: _____

Example: A: What are the hours for the clerk?
B: From 10:00 in the morning to 2:00 in the afternoon.

A: Where is the job?
B: It's at the bank.
A: What's the phone number?
B: It's 555-3233.

Student B: Ask about the jobs below.

A	B	C	D
Clerk Wanted Hrs. 10 A.M.–2 P.M. State Bank Call: 555-3233	Welders Hrs. 8 A.M.–4 P.M. _____ Call: 555-8423	Painter Hrs. _____ Ron's Paint Co. Call: _____	Cashiers Hrs. 2 P.M.–9 P.M. _____ Call: 555-6703

3 Group/Class Work

Step 1. Look for want ads in the newspaper or on bulletin boards. Write the information you find in the chart below.

	Job Title	Hours	Phone Number or Address
1.			
2.			
3.			
4.			

Step 2. Talk about the ads with the group. Which job do you like? Why? Tell the class.

4 Culture Work

Look at the pictures. The gesture is the same in both pictures. What do people do in these situations in your native country?

Unit 5
QUESTIONS AT AN INTERVIEW

Openers

Look at the picture. Point to these things:

an application   a Personnel Manager   a Social Security card

Where are they? What are they talking about?

1 Listen and Think

Listen to the conversation. Then check Yes or No.

	Yes	No
1. Does Mr. Martin want a job?		✔
2. Does Mei work at Quick Shop?		
3. Does Mr. Martin need cashiers?		
4. Can Mei start work on Friday?		

2 Talk to a Partner

Step 1. Practice the conversation with a partner.

A: What do you do now?
B: I'm **a painter**.
A: Where do you work?
B: I work at **Tom's Painting Service**.
A: Why do you want to change jobs?
B: I want to be **a custodian**.

Step 2. Change partners. Practice the conversation again. Use the jobs and workplaces in the pictures.

3 Read and Think

Step 1. Look at the pictures. Where is Mei?

Step 2. Read the text.

Now Mei Long works at Foodland Supermarket. She works part time from 8:00 in the morning to 1:00 in the afternoon. Now she can be with her younger sister and brother in the afternoon and then go to school in the evening.

Mei usually helps her sister study in the afternoon. Sometimes they go to the park. They often help their mother. They wash the clothes and help clean the house. Mei enjoys her new work schedule.

Step 3. Look at the vocabulary on the next page. Then read the text again.

Vocabulary

Daily Activities

get up

eat

drink

wash

write

watch

Work Times

Work Schedule		
Sunday		
Monday	7–11	
Tuesday	9:30–2:30	
Wednesday	4:00–9:00	
Thursday	10:00–4:00	
Friday		
Saturday		

part-time

Work Schedule		
Sunday		
Monday	9–5	
Tuesday	9–5	
Wednesday	9–5	
Thursday	9–5	
Friday	9–5	
Saturday		

full-time

Work Schedule	
Monday	8–4
Tuesday	8–4
Wednesday	8–4
Thursday	8–4
Friday	8–4

first shift
8:00 A.M.–4:00 P.M.
(morning–afternoon)

Work Schedule	
Monday	4–12
Tuesday	4–12
Wednesday	4–12
Thursday	4–12
Friday	4–12

second shift
4:00 P.M.–12:00 A.M.
(afternoon–night)

Work Schedule	
Monday	12–8
Tuesday	12–8
Wednesday	12–8
Thursday	12–8
Friday	12–8

third shift
12:00 A.M.–8:00 A.M.
(night–morning)

Word Match

Match the people and the activities.

1. I wash dishes.

2. They watch TV.

3. He eats at 12:00.

4. She gets up at 7:00.

5. We write in school.

6. She drinks coffee.

a.

b.

c.

d.

e.

f.

Practice

Listen and check the activities each person does.

	get up	eat	drink	wash	write	walk	study	go
Elena	✔							
Frank								
Mandy								
Ivan								

4 Put It in Writing

Write the answers.

Example: Where do you work now? *I work in a restaurant.*

1. Where do you work now? _____

2. What do you do now? _____

3. What job do you want? _____

4. Do you want to work full-time or part-time? _____

5. What's your Social Security number? _____

5 Listen and Speak

Step 1.   Listen.

A: Why do you want to change jobs?
B: I want to work **in the morning.**
A: I'm sorry. What did you say?
B: I want to work **in the morning.**

A: When can you start work?
B: I can start **on Monday.**
A: When?
B: **On Monday.**

Step 2.   Practice the conversations with a partner.

Step 3.   Change partners. Practice the conversations again. Use other times and days.

6 Read and Write

Step 1.   Read the information.

Application for Employment

Name _Carmen_   _Daniel_   _Lee_
         Last   First   Middle

Social Security No. _122-85-3242_

Position Desired:

    _____ housekeeper   ✔ janitor   _____ cashier   _____ wait staff

Time Available:

    _____ morning   ✔ afternoon   ✔ evening

    ✔ full-time   _____ part-time

Do you have a job now? ✔ Yes _____ No

Occupation _painter_

Employer and address _Tom's Painting Service, 48 Green Street, Chester_

Step 2.   Write the answers to the questions.

1. What's his name? _Daniel Lee Carmen._ _____

2. What's his Social Security Number? _____

3. What job does he want? _____

4. When does he want to work? _____

5. Does he want to work full-time or part-time? _____

6. What is his job now? _____

7. Where does he work now? _____

Step 3.   With a partner, compare your answers.

Form and Function

1 This job is good. I don't like that job.

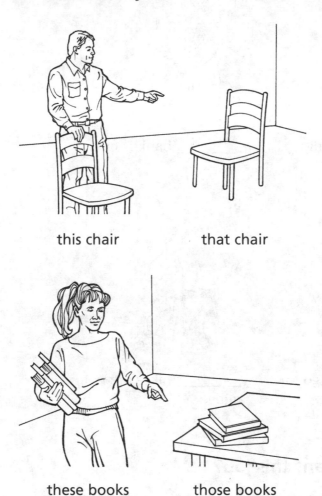

this chair   that chair

these books   those books

Examples

I like **this book.** I don't like **these books.**   I work at **that store.** We like to go to **those stores.**
Take **this paper.** Take **these papers.**   **That bag** is heavy. **Those bags** are heavy.

Practice 1

A. Listen. Circle the words you hear.

1. (this)   that   5. that   those

2. these   those   6. that   these

3. this   those   7. this   these

4. this   these   8. that   those

B. Fill in the missing words: *this*, *that*, *these*, *those*.

1.

___That___ car is nice.

2.

_____ bank is open.

3.

I like _____ book.

4.

_____ buses go to the hospital.

5.

_____ bikes are not mine.

6.

Do you need _____ papers?

2 Why do you want this job?

What do	I you we they	do?		Where do When	I you we they	work?
What does	he she it			Where does When	he she it	

Examples

Where do you **live?**
Why does she **go** to school?
When do they **eat?**
What time do we **study?**

I **live** in Smithtown.
Because she **wants** to study nursing.
They **eat** at 7:00.
We **study** at 5:30.

Practice 2

A. Listen. Circle the correct words.

1. What   Where   (When)   Why

2. What   Where   When   Why

3. What   Where   When   Why

4. What   Where   When   Why

5. What   Where   When   Why

6. What   Where   When   Why

B. Match the questions and answers.

1. Why do you like your job?   I work at a school.

2. What do you do at home?   I eat at 7:00 in the evening.

3. Where do you work?   She works in the evening.

4. When do you eat dinner?   She works in a restaurant.

5. When does Amy work?   At home I read.

6. Where does Amy work?   Because it's a good job.

C. Fill in the correct question word.

1. __Where__ does Anton work?   He works at the hotel.

2. _____ do you eat?   I eat at 8:00.

3. _____ is your job?   I am a bus driver.

4. _____ does she work?   She works the second shift.

5. _____ does Mary live?   She lives on Grand Street.

D. Work with a partner. Student A: Look at this page. Student B: Look at page 58. Ask a partner questions about the people. Fill in the missing information.

Example: B: **Where** does **Emma** work?
        A: **She** works in a **hospital.**

	Where?	When?	What?
Emma	hospital		nurse
Chad		2 P.M.–10 P.M.	cook
Peter and Mary	store		

Work with a partner. Student B: Look at this page. Student A: Look at page 57.
Ask your partner questions about the people. Fill in the missing information.

Example: A: **When** does **Emma** work?
B: **She** works from **6 A.M.** to **2 P.M.**

	Where?	**When?**	**What?**
Emma		6 A.M.–2 P.M.	
Chad	restaurant		
Peter and Mary		10 A.M.–7 P.M.	cashiers

E. Now write sentences. Use the information from the chart.

1. Emma _works in a hospital._ _____

2. She _____

3. She _____

4. Chad _____

5. He _____

6. He _____

7. Peter and Mary _____

8. They _____

9. They _____

F. Work with a partner. What do you like? What do you dislike? Why? Tell your partner one thing you like or dislike. Tell why.

Examples: A: I like my job.
B: Why?
A: Because it's interesting. I work with nice people.

B: I don't like my neighborhood.
A: Why?
B: Because it's far from my job.

Putting It to Work

1 Pair Work

Step 1.   Listen. Fill in the missing information on the form.

Application for Employment

Name ___Barton_____Sylvia_____Marie_____

             Last   First   Middle

Social Security No. _____

Position Desired:

_____ housekeeper _____ janitor _____ cashier _____ wait staff

Time Available:

_____ morning _____ afternoon _____ evening _____ full-time _____ part-time

---

Step 2.   Talk to a partner. Compare your answers.

2 Pair Work

Step 1.   Listen to the interview.

Mr. Martin:	What's your name?
Mei:	My name is Mei Long.
Mr. Martin:	What do you do?
Mei:	I'm a cashier.
Mr. Martin:	When can you work?
Mei:	I can work mornings.

Mr. Martin:	Do you want to work full-time or part-time?
Mei:	Part-time.
Mr. Martin:	I have an opening from 9 A.M. to 1 P.M. Are you interested?
Mei:	Yes, I am.

Step 2.   Student A: Look at this page. Student B: Look at page 60. Interview your partner. Circle the correct job.

Student A:

Job A
Gardener
8:00 A.M.–5:00 P.M.
Full time

Job B
Gardener
1:00 P.M.–5:00 P.M.

Now use this information to answer your partner's questions:

Your name is Bill Smith. You want to be a cook. You can work in the afternoon and in the evening. You want to work full-time.

Student B: Look at this page. Student A: Look at page 59.

Use this information to answer your partner's questions:

Your name is John Edwards. You want to be a gardener. You can work in the afternoon. You want to work part-time.

Now interview your partner. Circle the correct job.

Student B:

Job A	**Job B**
Cook	Cook
12:00 P.M.–4:00 P.M.	2:00 P.M.–10:00 P.M.
Part time	Full time

3 Group/Class Work

Step 1.   Interview three friends. Ask the questions below and write their answers.

	1	2	3
What's your name?	_____	_____	_____
What job do you want?	_____	_____	_____
Where do you work?	_____	_____	_____
When can you work?	_____	_____	_____

Step 2.   Talk about the answers with the group.

Step 3.   Tell the class your information.

4 Culture Work

Look at the pictures. What is different? What should you do at an interview?

Unit 6
JOB INSTRUCTIONS

Openers

Look at the picture. Point to these things:

a bed   a table   a sink
a mirror   a lamp   a mop

Where are they? What are they looking at? What are they talking about?

1 Listen and Think

Listen to the conversation. Then check Yes or No.

	Yes	No
1. Is this Ron's first day at work?	✔	
2. Does Ron clean the sink first?		
3. Does he vacuum the hall?		
4. Is Isabel going to help Ron?		

2 Talk to a Partner

Step 1. Practice the conversations with a partner.

A: Please **empty the wastebasket**.
B: **Empty the sink**?
A: No, **empty the wastebasket**.
B: Oh, all right.

A: **Clean the sink** and then **make the beds**.
B: **Clean the sink** and what?
A: **Make the beds**.

Step 2. Change partners. Practice the conversations
again. Use the checklist for the other chores.

> ROOM CLEANING CHECKLIST
>
> ☐ make the beds
> ☐ clean the sink
> ☐ empty the wastebasket
> ☐ wipe the tables
> ☐ vacuum the floor

3 Read and Think

Step 1. Look at the pictures. Ron is new on the job. And there's a lot of work.

Step 2. Read the text.

Ron is a new housekeeper. Isabel is
showing him the hotel rooms and the
cleaning supplies.

Ron has a cart with his supplies. He
has a sponge, a towel, and a vacuum
cleaner. The housekeeper cleans the sinks
and wipes the tables with the sponge and
the towel. He cleans the floors with the
vacuum cleaner.

Isabel is looking at the supplies. The
sponge is small. Ron needs a big sponge
for the tables.

Step 3. Look at the vocabulary on pages 63 and 64. Then read the text again.

Vocabulary

Work Equipment

mop

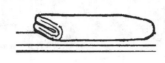
bucket

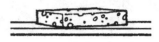
towel

sponge

Sizes

The pencil is **long**.

The pencil is **short**.

The bucket is **big**.

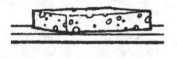

The sponge is **big**.

The sponge is **small**.

The bucket is **small**.

Direction Words

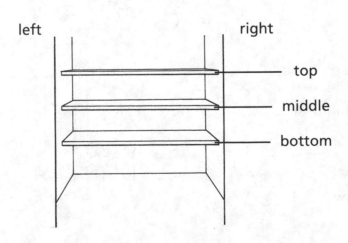

left   right   top   middle   bottom

Activities

put

take

give

count

open

close

Word Match

A. Match the sentences with the pictures.

1. Count the towels.

2. Take the bag.

3. Give me the mop.

4. Open the door.

5. Put the sponge in the sink.

6. Close the window.

a.

b.

c.

d.

e.

f.

B. Listen. Draw a line to show where the supplies should be.

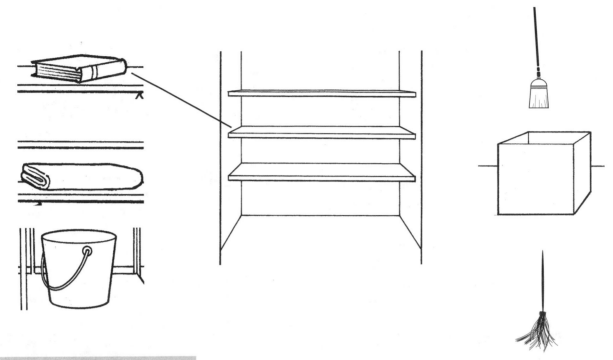

4 Put It in Writing

Look at the picture. Then complete the questions.

1. Where's the ___*sponge*___ ?   It's on the top shelf.

2. Where's the _____ ?   It's under the shelves.

3. Where's the _____ ?   It's on the cart.

4. Where's the _____ ?   It's on the middle shelf.

5. Where's the _____ ?   It's on the bottom shelf.

6. Where's the _____ ?   It's on the bottom shelf.

5 Listen and Speak

Step 1. Listen to the conversations.

A: Put **the sponge on the top shelf.**
B: Where?
A: **On the top shelf.**
B: OK.

A: I need **the mop.**
B: It's **on the cart.**
A: I'm sorry. What did you say?
B: It's **on the cart.**

Step 2. Practice the conversations with a partner.

Step 3. Practice the conversations again. Talk about other items in the picture.

6 Read and Write

Step 1. Read the information on the inventory list.

Supply Room Inventory List		Date: 6/22/97
Item	**Quantity**	**Location**
wastebaskets	6	bottom shelf
towels	22	middle shelf
plastic bags	1 box	top shelf
sponges	4	top shelf
vacuum	2	floor
supply cart	4	floor
buckets	3	bottom shelf

Step 2. Write the answers to the questions.

1. How many buckets are there? _*three.*_

2. Where is the vacuum? _____

3. Are there any brooms? _____

4. What is on the middle shelf? _____

5. What is in the box? _____

6. What is next to the bags on the top shelf? _____

Step 3. With a partner, compare answers.

Form and Function

1 We have one table and two chairs.

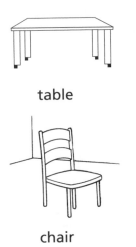

table

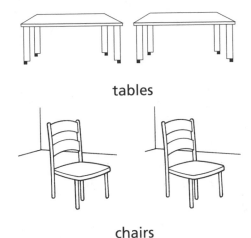

tables

chair

chairs

Examples

I have one **book.**
There is a **mop** on the **cart.**
Where is the **bank?**

We have three **books.**
There are some **mops** in the corner.
When are the **stores** open?

Practice 1

A. Listen. Circle the correct words.

1. bag   (bags)
2. vacuum   vacuums
3. bed   beds

4. towel   towels
5. cart   carts
6. room   rooms

B. Fill in the correct forms of the words.

1. There are three ___*windows*___ (window) in Room 36.

2. I need a _____ (broom).

3. Where is the _____ (bank)?

4. Are there any _____ (towel) on the cart?

5. Can you make those _____ (bed)?

6. I have a _____ (book).

2 These sponges are small. Those sponges are large.

The sponge is **dry**.

The sponge is **wet**.

The broom is **long**.

The broom is **short**.

A	**dry**	sponge.		An	**old**	book.
	wet			A	**new**	book.
	large					
	small					

Practice 2

A. Listen. Circle the words you hear.

1. (long)   large
2. short   small
3. old   small

4. short   old
5. light   wet
6. light   wet

B. With a partner, finish the sentences with *short, long, small,* or *large*.

1. The pencil is _____*short*_____ .

2. This is a _____ pencil.

3. These are _____ sponges.

4. This is a _____ bucket.

3 Open your books!

Open your books, please!

Examples

Come here!
Take that bag, please!

Put the box on the shelf!
First, **clean** the sink!

Practice 3

A. Listen. Circle the type of sentence you hear.

1. (!)   ?   2. !   ?   3. !   ?   4. !   ?   5. !   ?

B. Write a command for these actions.

1.

_____

2.

_____

3.

_____

4.

_____

4 Put it on the table.

Put	the book	on the table.	Put	the books	on the shelf.
	it			them	

Examples

Where's **the bag**?   I put **it** outside.
Do we need **these books**?   No, please take **them** home.

Practice 4

A. Listen. Circle the answer.

1. it (them)   **4.** it   them

2. it   them   **5.** it   them

3. it   them   **6.** it   them

B. Fill in the missing words in the conversations. Use *it* or *them*.

1. A: Please give me three brooms.

  B: OK. I have ____*them*____ on the cart.

2. A: Can Ron clean that window?

  B: Yes, he can clean _____ .

3. A: Where do I put this bag?

  B: Put _____ outside.

4. A: Do we clean the sinks first?

  B: Yes, we clean _____ first.

5. A: Where is the sponge?

  B: I have _____ .

6. A: Are the papers in the office?

  B: Yes, I put _____ there.

Putting It to Work

1 Pair Work

Work with a partner. Look at the picture. Tell your partner where to put things. Then write them in the correct places.

Student A: **Tell your partner about these things:**

papers   vacuum   wastebasket   books   bags

Student B: **Tell your partner about these things:**

box   sponge   pens   towels   bucket

Example: A Put the papers on
the bottom shelf
B: OK.

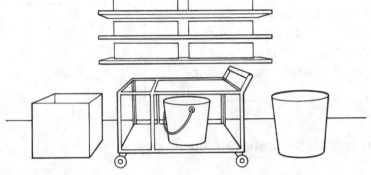

2 Pair Work

Step 1.   Tell your partner what to do. Student A: Look at this page. Student B: Look at page 72.

Student A: Tell your partner
what to do in Room 220.

Now listen. Your partner will tell you what to do in Room 214. Check the things to do.

Work Order: Room 220

- empty the wastebaskets
- put towels in the bathroom
- clean the sink
- vacuum the floor
- wipe the tables

Work Order: Room 214

_____ clean the sink
_____ wash the windows
_____ wipe the tables
_____ empty the wastebaskets
_____ put the bag outside
_____ vacuum the floor
_____ make the beds
_____ put towels in the bathroom
_____ wash the floor
_____ put the books on the shelf

Step 2.   Talk to your partner. Compare your answers.

Student B: Look at this page. **Student A:** Look at page 71.

Listen. Your partner will tell you
what to do in Room 220.
Check the things to do.

Now tell your
partner what to do in Room 214.

Work Order: Room 220

_____ clean the sink
_____ wash the windows
_____ wipe the tables
_____ empty the wastebaskets
_____ put the bag outside
_____ vacuum the floor
_____ make the beds
_____ put towels in the bathroom
_____ wash the floor
_____ put the books on the shelf

Work Order: Room 214

• put the bag outside
• wash the windows
• put the books on the shelf
• make the beds
• wash the floor

Talk to your partner. Compare your answers.

3 Group/Class Work

With a group, read the work order. Then make a list of the things you need to do this work.
Talk about your list with the class.

Work Order: Room 315

• clean the sink   • vacuum the floor
• wash the windows   • make the beds
• wipe the tables   • put towels in the bathroom
• empty the wastebaskets   • wash the floor

What do you need?

_____

_____

_____

_____

_____

4 Culture Work

Sometimes you say something,
but people don't understand.
What can you do?

Unit 7
MONEY, PRICES, AND PAYCHECKS

Openers

Look at the picture. Point to these things:

a vending machine   a sandwich   soda

Where are they? What are they doing? What are they talking about?

1 Listen and Think

Listen to the conversation. Then check Yes or No.

	Yes	No
1. Is Carlos getting a soda?	_____	✔
2. Is Mike getting a sandwich?	_____	_____
3. Does Mike need change?	_____	_____
4. Does Carlos have change for a dollar?	_____	_____

2 Talk to a Partner

Step 1. Practice the conversations with a partner.

A: I'd like **an apple,** please.
B: That's **forty-five cents.**
A: Here you are. Thanks.
B: Thank you.

A: How much is **a sandwich?**
B: **Two dollars.**
A: I'd like **a sandwich** and **an apple.**
B: That's **two dollars and forty-five cents.**
A: Here you are.
B: Thanks.

Step 2. Change partners. Practice the conversations again. Use the menu for other orders.

3 Read and Think

Step 1. Look at the picture. Carlos gets his paycheck on Fridays.

Step 2. Read the text.

Carlos works at Taylor Department Store. He's a sales clerk. Carlos usually brings his lunch to work. Sometimes he buys a snack at work.

On Fridays, Carlos gets his paycheck. During lunch, Carlos takes his check to the bank. On Fridays, he likes to eat his lunch in the park near the bank.

Step 3. Read the text again. Underline all the time expressions in the text. With a partner, compare your work.

Vocabulary

Money

Coins

a penny
one cent
1¢
$00.01

a nickel
five cents
5¢
$00.05

a dime
ten cents
10¢
$00.10

a quarter
twenty-five cents
25¢
$00.25

Bills

one dollar
$1.00

five dollars
$5.00

ten dollars
$10.00

twenty dollars
$20.00

Prices

$2.00

$2.10

$2.50

$2.00
two dollars

$2.10
two dollars and ten cents

$2.50
two dollars and fifty cents

Word Match

A. Draw a line from the prices to the words on the machine.

Washing Machine $.85
Dryer $.50

B. Listen. Circle the prices you hear.

1. $0.17 $0.70   ($0.79)   5. $5.25 $4.20 $5.75

2. $2.15 $2.50 $2.55   6. $17.10 $7.70 $16.70

3. $9.85 $8.95 $9.95   7. $4.65 $4.55 $5.65

4. $3.79 $3.69 $3.19   8. $12.18 $12.80 $20.80

C. Match the prices with the amounts.

1. $0.85

2. $0.70

3. $2.15

4. $5.75

5. $1.45

6. $3.80

7. $2.55

8. $2.30

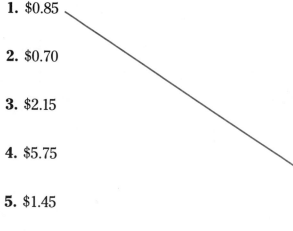

Money, Prices, and Paychecks

4 Put It in Writing

Step 1. Read the information on the store ads. Write the answers to the questions.

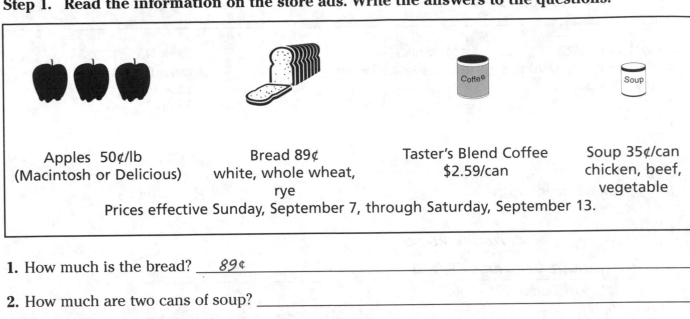

Apples 50¢/lb
(Macintosh or Delicious)

Bread 89¢
white, whole wheat,
rye

Taster's Blend Coffee
$2.59/can

Soup 35¢/can
chicken, beef,
vegetable

Prices effective Sunday, September 7, through Saturday, September 13.

1. How much is the bread? __*89¢*_____

2. How much are two cans of soup? _____

3. How much are the apples? _____

4. How much is 2 lbs. of apples? _____

5. How much is a can of coffee and 2 lbs. of apples? _____

5 Listen and Speak

Step 1. Listen to the conversation.

A: Can I help you?
B: Yes, please. I'd like **a hamburger and coffee.**
A: **A hamburger and coffee.** That'll be **$3.00.**
B: Here's **$5.00.**
A: OK, your change is **$1.00.**
B: Wait, excuse me, that's the wrong change.
A: No, it's correct.
B: No, it's not. **This is one dollar.** You owe
   me **another dollar.**
A: Oh, you're right. Sorry. Here you are.

Menu

Hamburger $2.00
Salad $1.00
Soup   95¢
Apple   45¢
Coffee $1.00
Tea   75¢

Step 2. Practice the conversation with a partner.

Step 3. Now practice the conversation again with the items and prices on the menu.
Check the change your partner gives you.

6 Read and Write

Step 1.   Read the paycheck.

Dept. No. 2513	Dept. Sales	Check No. 018023
Period Ending 03/03/96	Employee No. 054255	Name Carlos Ramirez
Regular Hours	Overtime	Gross Pay
40	——	360.00
Fed. W/H	FICA	State W/H	Net Pay
24.58	27.54	6.22	301.66

Taylor Department Store   No.   018023
42 Southside Boulevard
Williston, MA
Pay to the Order of *Carlos Ramirez* $ 301.66
          Three hundred one and 66/100   Dollars
Chemical Trust Bank
Williston, MA

          Joseph Stanton

:011600582:   34911631   018023

Step 2.   Write the answers.

1. Whose check is this? _____

2. Where does he work? _____

3. How many hours does he work? _____

4. How much is his gross pay? _____

5. How much is his check? _____

Step 3.   With a partner, compare your answers.

Form and Function

1 Some coffee and a sandwich, please.

an apple
one apple

coffee
one cup of coffee

some apples
two apples

some coffee
two cups of coffee

Examples

I want **a sandwich**.
There are **three quarters** on **the table**.
Where are **the machines**?

We want **soup**, please.
There is **some money** on the table.
Where is **the bread**?

Practice 1

A. Listen for these words. Add an -s if it is needed.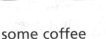

1. coffee_____

2. dime_____

3. pencil_____

4. water_____

5. paper_____

6. tea_____

7. mop_____

8. soap_____

9. money_____

B. Fill in the correct forms of the words.

1. May I have five _____*apples*_____ (apple)?

2. Do you want some _____ (coffee)?

3. I need some _____ (dime) for the machine.

4. Are there any _____ (book) on the table?

5. There is some _____ (soup) in the kitchen.

6. Put some _____ (water) on the stove, please.

2 How much sugar do you have? How many apples are you buying?

How many <u>apples</u> are there?	**How much** <u>water</u> is there?
There are a lot of <u>apples</u>.	There is a lot of <u>water</u>.

Examples

How many **quarters** do you need? We need a lot of **quarters**.
How much **money** does she want? She wants a lot of **money**.

Practice 2

A. Listen. Circle the question words you hear.

1. how much   (how many)   4. how much   how many
2. how much   how many   5. how much   how many
3. how much   how many   6. how much   how many

B. Complete the sentences with *how much* or *how many*.

1. A: There are a lot of apples in the refrigerator. B: Really? ___*How many*___ are there?

2. _____ time do you have today? I want to talk to you about your paycheck.

3. _____ people do you know in Massachusetts?

4. _____ money do you have on you right now?

5. A: This TV is very expensive. B: Really? _____ do you want to spend?

6. A: I need more time. B: OK, _____ time do you need?

7. This is the wrong change. I have three quarters, two dimes, and a nickel. B: _____ quarters do you need?

8. A: _____ bread do you want? B: Oh, just a small slice, please.

3 That's the wrong change. You owe me another dollar.

You	owe	**me**	a dollar.		You	owe	**us**	a quarter.
		him					**them**	
		her						
		(it)						

Examples

Excuse me, that's wrong. You **owe me** another quarter. You **owe me** another fifteen cents.
A: Wait, that's the wrong change. You **owe me** some more money.
B: No, I don't. I don't **owe you** any money.
They **owe us** a lot of money. We **owe them** ten dollars. You **owe her** three dollars.

Practice 3

A. Listen. Circle the words you hear.

1. (owe me)   owe him

2. owe them   owe him

3. owe him   owe me

4. owe me   owe you

5. owe you   owe us

6. owe me   owe you

B.   With a partner, play the roles of a cashier and a customer. The cashier gives the wrong change. How much more change does the cashier owe? The customer tells the cashier. Follow the model and change roles.

Student A: Look at this page.
Student B: Look at page 82.

B: **Two cans of soup?** That's **seventy-eight cents,** please.
A: Here you are.
B: Out of **a dollar? Twelve cents** is your change.
A: No, that's the wrong change. You owe me another **ten cents.**
B: Oh, you're right. Sorry. Here you are.
A: Thank you.

Role 1: Student A—*Cashier*—You sell:

2 apples	A quart of milk	12 eggs
Total price: $0.22	Total price: $1.59	Total price: $0.79
Receive: $1.00	Receive: $2.00	Receive: $1.00
Give back: 60 cents	Give back: 20 cents	Give back: 10 cents

Role 2: Student A—*Customer*—You buy:

2 cans of soup	3 apples	A loaf of bread
Total price: $0.78	Total price: $0.33	Total price: $0.49
Give: $1.00	Give: $5.00	Give: $0.75
Change: _____	Change: _____	Change: _____

With a partner, play the roles of a cashier and a customer. The cashier gives the wrong change. How much more change does the cashier owe? The customer tells the cashier. Follow the model and change roles.

Student B: Look at this page.
Student A: Look at page 81.

B: **Two cans of soup?** That's **seventy-eight cents,** please.

A: Here you are.

B: Out of a **dollar? Twelve cents** is your change.

A: No, that's the wrong change. You owe me another **ten cents.**

B: Oh, you're right. Sorry. Here you are.

A: Thank you.

Role 1: Student B—*Customer*—You buy:

2 apples	A quart of milk	12 eggs
Total price: $0.22	Total price: $1.59	Total price: $0.79
Give: $1.00	Give: $2.00	Give: $1.00
Change: _____	Change: _____	Change: _____

Role 2: Student B—*Cashier*—You sell:

2 cans of soup	3 apples	A loaf of bread
Total price: $0.78	Total price: $0.33	Total price: $0.49
Receive: $1.00	Receive: $5.00	Receive: $0.75
Give back: $0.12	Give back: $2.00	Give back: $0.20

C. Complete the conversations with the following words in the correct places.

how much/how many   owe   some   any   a   an

1. A: Do you have ____*any*____ apples?

   B: Sure. _____ would you like?

   A: _____ do they cost?

   B: Ten cents each. They're on sale.

   A: OK, I'll have ten, please.

   B: All right, ten apples. That's $1.08.

   A: Here you are.

   B: Out of two dollars? Ninety-two cents is your change.

   A: This is eighty-two cents. You _____ me another ten cents.

   B: Oh, sorry. Here you are.

2. A: I'd like _____ coffee, please.

   B: Here you are. That's seventy-two cents, please.

   A: Here you are.

   B: Out of _____ dollar? OK, here's your change.

   A: This is the wrong change.

   B: No, it's not. It's correct.

   A: No, it's wrong. This is _____ nickel and three cents. You _____ me another twenty cents.

   B: Oh, sorry. Here you are.

Putting It to Work

1 Pair Work

Step 1. Listen and fill in the missing prices and quantities.

Item	Unit Price	Quantity	Total Price
apples	_35¢_ each	4	_$1.40_
milk	_____	1 gallon	_____
bread	_____	_____ loaves	_____
grapes	_____ /lb.	1 lb.	_____
bananas	_____ /lb.	2 lbs.	_____
pears	_____ /lb.	_____ lbs.	_____
coffee	_____ /cup	3 cups	_____
		TOTAL	_____

Step 2. Then work with a partner to calculate the total prices.

2 Pair Work

Ask a friend what he or she would like. Each person has $10. Calculate the total amount of each order and the change.

SNACK BAR					
Sandwich	ham & cheese	2.25	Fruit	apple	.50
	tuna			orange	
	chicken salad			banana	
	vegetarian				
			Salad	small	1.25
	Soup chicken	1.10		large	2.50
	vegetable			Cookies	.95
Coffee		.75		Soda	.80
Tea		.75		Iced Tea	.85
Milk		.80			

_____   TOTAL _____

_____   Change _____

_____

3 Group/Class Work

Step 1. Go to two stores. Compare the prices of different items. Write the items and prices on the list.

Store 1: _____	Store 2: _____
apples _____	apples _____
milk _____	milk _____
_____	_____
_____	_____
_____	_____
_____	_____

Step 2. Compare prices for different items. Talk about the differences in prices. Which store do you think has better prices? Where do you shop? Why?

4 Culture Work

Look at the pictures. Talk about the situations. Which is the better way to disagree? Why? What can you say if there is a mistake with money?

Unit 8
SAFETY SIGNS AND WARNINGS

Openers

Look at the picture. Point to these things:

a fire   an Emergency Exit   an alarm
a fire extinguisher   smoke   a telephone

Where are they? What is happening? What can they do?

1 Listen and Think

Listen to the conversation. Then check Yes or No.

	Yes	No
1. Is Mr. Timmons a fire fighter?	_____	✔
2. Is there a lot of smoke?	_____	_____
3. Is Anton all right?	_____	_____
4. Is Anton going to put out the fire?	_____	_____

2 Talk to a Partner

Step 1. Practice the conversation with a partner.

A: Help!
B: What's the problem?
A: There's a fire **in the hall!**
B: Get out. I'll call 911.

Step 2. Change partners. Practice the conversation again. Talk about the other rooms in the house.

3 Read and Think

Step 1. Look at the picture. There's a fire at the company.

Step 2. Read the text.

Mr. Timmons is calling 911. The emergency operator is asking him questions. Mr. Timmons is telling the operator the address and location of the fire in the building.

The operator is sending help. She's sending fire trucks and an ambulance. The fire fighters are going to put out the fire. The ambulance workers are going to help people who are hurt. Mr. Timmons is checking the building to make sure everyone is out.

Step 3. Look at the vocabulary on the next page. Then read the text again.

Vocabulary

Parts of the Body

ear   eye   head   neck   back   arm   hand   leg   knee   foot

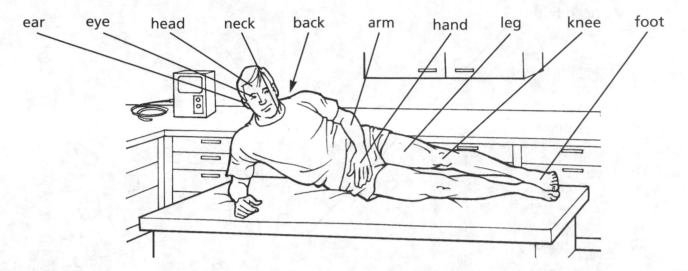

Warning Signs

No Smoking

Exit

Poison

Radiation

High Voltage

Hard Hat Area

Emergency Words

Fire

Accident

Emergency

Ambulance

Police

Fire Department

Word Match

A. Match the words with the parts of the body.

1. My head hurts.

2. His leg hurts.

3. His ear hurts.

4. Her arm hurts.

5. My foot hurts.

6. Her back hurts.

a.

b.

c.

d.

e.

f.

B. Write the signs in the places where they belong.

Poison	Radiation	High Voltage
Emergency Exit	No Smoking	Fire Extinguisher

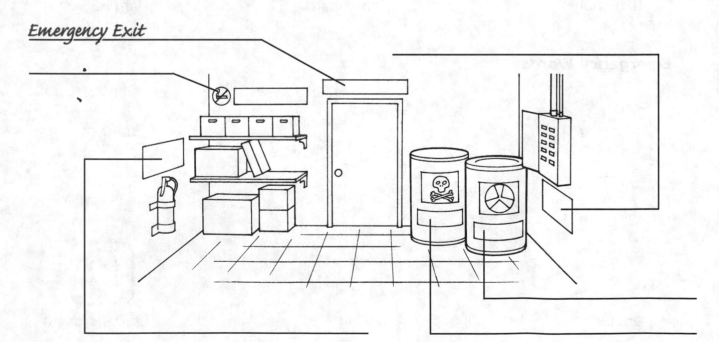

Emergency Exit

4 Put It in Writing

Look at the picture and answer the 911 operator's questions.

911: What's the matter?   You: _____

911: What's the address?   You: _____

911: Where is it in the building? You: _____

911: Is anyone hurt?   You: _____

5 Listen and Speak

Step 1. Listen.

      A: Watch out!
      B: Oh, no!
      A: What's the matter?
      B: My **head** hurts.
      A: I'm calling the supervisor!

Step 2. Practice the conversation with a partner.

Step 3. Change partners. Practice the conversation again using other parts of the body.

6 Read and Write

Step 1. Read the information on the accident report form.

Accident Report Form

Date: _5/22/96_   Time: _10:15_ A.M./P.M.   Location: _kitchen_

Name of injured person: _Sam Walters_   Dept. _Banquet_

Nature of injury: _Sprained foot, slipped on wet floor_

Action taken: Hospital _✔_   First Aid _____   Home _____

Other:_____

Person reporting accident: _Jean Addams_

Step 2. Write the answers to the questions.

1. Who is hurt? _____ _Sam Walters._ _____

2. What is the date? _____

3. What time was the accident? _____

4. Where was the accident? _____

5. What did Sam hurt? _____

6. Did Sam go to the hospital? _____

7. Who reported the accident? _____

Step 3. With a partner, compare your answers.

Form and Function

1 A: What are you doing? B: I'm calling 911.

I **am**	call**ing**.	Am I	call**ing**?
You **are**		Are you	
He **is**		Is he	
She **is**		Is she	
We **are**		Are we	
They **are**		Are they	

Examples

I**'m going** outside now.

She**'s working** in the kitchen right now.

They**'re washing** the windows.

Are you **coming** with me?

Is she **talking** to the supervisor?

Are they **taking** a break?

Practice 1

A. Listen. Circle the correct words.

1. call   (calling)
2. read   reading
3. eat   eating

4. help   helping
5. listen   listening
6. get   getting

B. Fill in the correct forms of the words.

1. He ____*is*____ ____*pulling*____ (pull) the fire alarm.

2. They _____ _____ (eat) lunch.

3. I _____ _____ (go) outside now.

4. _____ Mary_____ (check) the rooms?

5. We _____ _____ (open) the windows.

6. _____ you _____ (wait) for me?

7. _____ they _____ (call) for help?

8. She _____ _____ (read) the paper.

C. What are the people doing in the pictures? Tell a partner.

2 Don't do that!

Open the box!	**Don't** open the box!

Examples

Come here!

Take that bag, please!

Put the box on the shelf!

Don't go there!

Don't take that!

Don't put the box on the shelf!

Practice 2

A. Listen. Circle the command you hear.

1. Run   (Don't run)
2. Go   Don't go
3. Push   Don't push

4. Close   Don't close
5. Lock   Don't lock
6. Touch   Don't touch

B. Write a command for these actions.

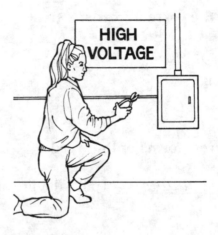

1. _____

2. _____

3. _____

4. _____

C. Tell a friend what to do or not to do about these signs:

DANGER

3 How often? How much? How many?

How often?	every day, never, once a day, twice a week
How many?	5 or 6 (apples, books, chairs . . .)
How much?	a lot of, one cup of, a little (coffee, water, tea . . .)

Examples

How often do you work?   I work **every day.**
How many hours do you work?   I work **8 hours a day.**
How much coffee do you want?   I want **two cups of coffee.**

Practice 3

A. Listen. Circle the correct answer.

1. (twice a day)   two days
2. every day   five hours
3. once a week   one cup

4. twice a week   one day
5. eight   a lot
6. once a month   a little

B. Work with a partner. Student A: Look at this page. Student B: Look at page 94. Ask questions and fill in the missing information.

B: **How often** does Ed work?
A: He works **five days a week.**
B: How often do you work?
A: I work _____.

How often does/do . . . ?	Marie	Ed	You
work		5 days a week	
watch TV	every day		
go to the store		once a week	
read the newspaper	twice a week		

Work with a partner. Student B: Look at this page. Student A: Look at page 93. Ask questions and fill in the missing information.

A: **How often** does
    Marie work?
B: She works **three**
    days a week.
A: How often do
    you work?
B: I work

    _____.

How often does/do . . . ?	Marie	Ed	You
work	3 days a week		
watch TV		never	
go to the store	once a day		
read the newspaper		every day	

C. Now complete the questions and answers with the information from the chart.

1. How often _____ Marie work? She works _____.

2. How often _____ Ed work? He _____.

3. How often _____ you work? I _____.

4. How often _____ your partner work? _____.

5. How often _____ Marie _____ TV? She _____.

6. How often _____ Ed _____ TV? He _____.

7. How often _____ Marie _____ to the store? She _____.

8. How often _____ Ed _____ to the store? He _____.

9. How often _____ Marie _____ the newspaper? She _____.

10. How often _____ Ed _____ the newspaper? He _____.

_____

_____

D. Write the other questions about your partner and yourself on a separate sheet of paper.

Example: A: How often do you watch TV? B: I _____.

Putting It to Work

1 Pair Work

Step 1. Listen. Check things to do or not to do when there is a fire.

Do	Don't	
____	✔	try to put the fire out by yourself
____	____	pull the fire alarm
____	____	tell everyone to go outside
____	____	run
____	____	call 911
____	____	tell the operator your address
____	____	try to get anything
____	____	go back inside the building

Step 2. With a partner, talk about other fire safety rules you know.

2 Pair Work

Step 1. Listen to the conversation.

A: 911, Emergency. What's the problem?

B: There's **a fire** here! Come quickly!

A: What's the address?

B: **8224 Hatfield Road, Santa Cruz.**

A: OK, is anyone hurt?

B: I don't know.

A: OK, what's your name?

B: **Tim Smith.**

A: What's your phone number?

B: **822-3764.**

Step 2. Play two roles: (1) Report an emergency, and (2) Take an emergency call.

Student A: Look at this page. Student B: Look at page 96.

Role 1: Student A—Report these details to 911:

What: A two-car crash
Where: The street your school is on
Injured: Two people

Type of emergency	
Address	
Anyone hurt?	
Caller's name	

Role 2: Student A—You are the 911 operator. Fill out the 911 Emergency report form.

Play two roles: (1) Report an emergency, and (2) Take an emergency call.

Student B: Look at this page. Student A: Look at page 95.

Role 1: Student B—You are the 911 operator. Answer the phone. Your partner is going to report an emergency. Fill out the 911 Emergency report form.

Role 2: Student B—Report these details to 911:

What: A car accident
Where: The street your school is on
Injured: One person

Type of emergency	
Address	
Anyone hurt?	
Caller's name	

3 Group/Class Work

With some friends, find emergency phone numbers for your area. Call and report an emergency. Keep this list near your telephone.

EMERGENCY PHONE NUMBERS

FIRE _____
AMBULANCE _____
POLICE _____
POISON CONTROL _____
DOCTOR/CLINIC _____
NEIGHBOR _____
OTHER _____

4 Culture Work

What do you do in an emergency?

Who can help you learn what to do? Who can help at work? Who can help at your home or apartment building?

Unit 9
SKILLS FOR THE JOB

Look at the picture. Point to these things:

a computer   a calculator   a copy machine
a file cabinet   a printer

Where are they? What are they talking about?

1 Listen and Think

Listen to the conversation. Then check Yes or No.

	Yes	No
1. Does Amy want to be a secretary?	_____	✔
2. Was Amy a receptionist at a school?	_____	_____
3. Was she a receptionist for four years?	_____	_____
4. Can Amy type?	_____	_____

2 Talk to a Partner

Step 1. Practice the conversation with a partner.

A: Hi. I'm **Paul**. Are you new here?
B: Yes, I am. My name is **Rita**. I'm
   the new **receptionist**.
A: Nice to meet you.
B: Can you use this **copy machine**?
A: Yes, I can. Do you need some help?
B: Yes, thanks.

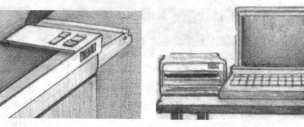

Step 2. Change partners. Practice the conversation again.
Talk about the other jobs and machines.

3 Read and Think

Step 1. Look at the picture. Amy is filling out a job application. She is writing about her skills.

Step 2. Read the text.

Amy is filling out an application for a job. There are many questions about her work experience. First she writes about her present job. She is a receptionist at the Proctor Bank. She started there in 1995. Next, she writes about her past job. She was a child-care worker from 1993 to 1995.

Amy has many skills. She can type and use a computer. She can drive, and she can speak Spanish. In addition, Amy likes to work with people.

Step 3. Read the text again. Circle the words for Amy's jobs. Underline the words for her skills.

Vocabulary

Skills

sew

type

fix cars

drive

cut hair

mix drinks

paint

file

Transportation

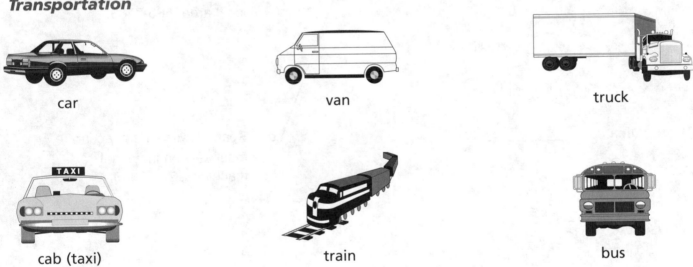

car

van

truck

cab (taxi)

train

bus

Word Match

A. Look at the pictures. Then find the ads with the correct skills. Match the pictures with the ads.

1. Sara can ___*sew*___.

2. Hector can _____.

3. Irene likes to _____ hair.

4. Allen can _____ cars.

5. Tuan can _____ fast.

a. **Mechanic Needed**
To fix foreign cars. Need own tools. 921-3321.

b. **Secretary**—Must type 70 wpm. Computer exp. helpful. 484-3985.

c. **Delivery driver**—to drive van, deliver packages. Must know local area. 566-7466.

d. **Seamstress**—Fast, accurate, must sew on industrial machines. 731-2300.

e. **Hairdresser Needed**
For stylish salon to cut hair, style, give perms. 566-0775.

4 Put It in Writing

Write about your work experience.

Work Experience		
Present Job		
Job Title	Place	Dates
		From
		To
Past Jobs		
Job Title	Place	Dates
		From
		To
		From
		To
		From
		To

5 Listen and Speak

Step 1. Listen to the conversation.

A: What experience do you have?
B: Well, I'm a **bookkeeper**. I work at the **hospital**.
A: Can you **type**?
B: Yes, I can.
A: Good. What else can you do?
B: I can **file** and **use a computer**.

Step 2. Practice the conversation with a partner.

Step 3. Change partners. Practice the conversation again using other jobs and skills.

6 Read and Write

Step 1. Read the information on the application.

Work Application Form

Name _Eric Holas_   **Social Security No.** _412-55-9771_

Address _84 Chestnut St., Springfield, MA_   **Telephone** _484-6223_

Desired Job: _Bookkeeper_

Work experience: (Start with present job.)

Job Title	Employer	Address	Dates
Bookkeeper	Taylor Dept. Store	200 South St., Springfield	From 1995 to present
Waiter	Springfield Inn	4112 Main St., Springfield	From 1993 to 1995

Skills: (Please check all that apply.)

_____ type   ✔ drive   ✔ keep books

_____ use computer   _____ sew   ✔ file

Step 2. Write the answers to the questions.

1. What job does Eric want? _He wants to be a bookkeeper._

2. Where does he work now? _____

3. What is his job now? _____

4. When was he a waiter? _____

5. Can Eric keep books? _____

6. What other skills does he have? _____

Step 3. With a partner, compare your answers.

Form and Function

1 I can drive very well.

I **can** drive.

He **cannot (can't)** drive.

Examples

He's a mechanic. He **can fix** cars.
I'm a cook. I **can't fix** cars.
They're bus drivers. They **can drive** a bus.
We're housekeepers. We **cannot drive** a bus.

Practice 1

A. Listen. Circle the words you hear and match them with the skills.

1. can   (can't)   **a.** fix the car

2. can   can't   **b.** carry the bags

3. can   can't   **c.** sew

4. can   can't   **d.** drive a truck

5. can   can't   **e.** use a computer

6. can   can't   **f.** paint

7. can   can't   **g.** type

8. can   can't   **h.** cut hair

B. Check your skills. Then fill in the missing words in the sentences.

	sew	paint	cook	drive	type	fix cars
Mark		✔	✔	✔	✔	
Emma	✔		✔	✔		✔
(you)						

1. Mark _____*can't*_____ sew.

2. He _____ paint.

3. Mark _____ type.

4. Emma _____ fix cars.

5. She _____ type.

6. Emma _____ paint.

7. Mark and Emma _____ drive.

8. I _____ cook.

9. I can _____ .

10. I can't _____ .

C. What can you do? What can't you do? Think of two things. Then tell a partner.

Example: I can speak Spanish. I can type. I can't speak Chinese.

2   I was a mechanic in Peru.

I	**was** . . .	I	**wasn't** . . .	(Where)	**Was**	I . . .
You	**were** . . .	You	**weren't** . . .		**Were**	you . . .
He	**was** . . .	He	**wasn't** . . .		**Was**	he . . .
She	**was** . . .	She	**wasn't** . . .		**Was**	she . . .?
We	**were** . . .	We	**weren't** . . .		**Were**	we . . .
They	**were** . . .	They	**weren't** . . .		**Were**	they . . .

Examples

I **was** a secretary for three years.
Was he a waiter?   Yes, he **was** a waiter in Poland.
Were they janitors?   No, they **weren't**.

Practice 2

A. Listen. Circle the correct words.

1. was   were
2. wasn't   weren't
3. was   were

4. wasn't   weren't
5. was   were
6. wasn't   weren't

B. Fill in the correct forms of the verb: *was, were.*

1. I _____was_____ a waiter at the Jade Garden Restaurant.

2. How long _____ you a waiter?

3. I _____ a waiter for two years.

4. My father _____ a cook from 1989 to 1994.

5. My brothers _____ mechanics at Tony's Garage.

6. _____ your sister a bookkeeper?

7. No, she _____ n't.

C. Work with a partner. Student A: Look at this page. Student B: Look at page 106.

All of the people below live and work in Seattle now. But in 1993, some of them were in different cities. And their jobs were different.

Ask your partner questions about these people. Fill in the missing information.

Example:

     B: Was **Ronald** in Seattle in 1993?
     A: No, **he wasn't.**
     B: Where was **he**?
     A: **He was in Los Angeles.**
     B: Was **he a musician** then?
     A: No, **he was a cook.**

Person	Now	1993
Ronald	Musician, Seattle	Cook, Los Angeles
Susan	Bookkeeper, Seattle	
Peter	Teacher, Seattle	Mechanic, San Francisco
Melissa	Nurse, Seattle	
Jack	Sales Clerk, Seattle	Cashier, Seattle
Barbara	Fire Fighter, Seattle	
Your Partner		

Work with a partner. Student B: Look at this page. Student A: Look at page 105.

All of the people below live and work in Seattle now. But in 1993, they were in different cities. And their jobs were different.

Ask your partner questions about these people. Fill in the missing information.

Example:

A: Was **Susan** in Seattle in 1993?
B: No, **she wasn't**.
A: Where was **she**?
B: **She was in New Orleans**.
A: Was **she a bookkeeper** then?
B: No, **she was a waitress**.

Person	Now	1993
Ronald	Musician, Seattle	
Susan	Bookkeeper, Seattle	Waitress, New Orleans
Peter	Teacher, Seattle	
Melissa	Nurse, Seattle	Receptionist, Houston
Jack	Sales Clerk, Seattle	
Barbara	Fire Fighter, Seattle	Secretary, Portland
Your Partner		

D. Complete the sentences below. Use the information from the chart.

1. Ronald is a musician in Seattle now. In 1993, he _was a cook in Los Angeles_.

2. Susan is a bookkeeper in Seattle now. In 1993, she _____.

3. Peter is a teacher in Seattle now. In 1993, he _____.

4. Melissa is a nurse in Seattle now. In 1993, she _____.

5. Jack is a sales clerk in Seattle now. In 1993, he _____.

6. Barbara is a fire fighter in Seattle now. In 1993, she _____.

7. My partner is _____ now.

   In 1993, _____.

E. Write about yourself.

I am _____ now.

In 1993, I _____.

Putting It to Work

1 Pair Work

Step 1. Listen to the conversation.

Application Form

Name _Pierre Dupuy_   Soc. Sec. No. _____

Address _41A Church St., Woodbury, NY_   Telephone _____

Desired Job: _Maintenance_

Work experience: (Start with present job.)

Job Title	Employer	Address	Dates
	Edson Car Repair Shop	110 Main St., Woodbury, NY	From _____ To _present_
	Doyle Paint Co.	75 Redwood Dr.	From _____ To _1994_

Skills: (Please check all that apply.)

____ type   ____ drive   ____ fix sinks   ____ paint

Step 2. With a partner, complete the form.

2 Pair Work

Step 1. Listen to the conversation.

A: What's your name?
B: My name is **Carol Severs**.
A: What job do you want?
B: I want to be a **cook**.

A: What experience do you have?
B: I was **a cook from 1994 to 1996**.
A: Where was that?
B: At **the Boston Cafe**.

Step 2. Practice the conversation with a partner. Use your own information. Complete the form with your partner's answers.

Name _____

Job Desired _____

Work Experience:

Job Title	Employer	Dates

3 Group/Class Work

Step 1. Look at the list below. In a group, talk about your skills. Mark them on the list.

Step 2. What jobs or workplaces use the skills below? Mark them on the chart.

Skills	Jobs	Workplaces
drive		
cook		
sew		
fix a sink		
use a computer		
grow plants		
speak Spanish		
use a calculator		
fix cars		
use a copy machine		

Step 3. Share your answers with the class.

4 Culture Work

Do men or women do these jobs in your native country?

What jobs can men do in the United States? What jobs can women do?

Unit 10
MAY I TAKE A MESSAGE?

Openers

Look at the picture. Point to these things:

a calendar   a clock
a stapler   an appointment book

Where are they? What are they talking about?

1 Listen and Think

Listen to the conversation. Then check Yes or No.

	Yes	No
1. Is Les Green a doctor?	_____	_____
2. Is Isabel sick?	_____	_____
3. Is the appointment on Tuesday?	_____	_____
4. Is the appointment at 4:00?	_____	_____

2 Talk to a Partner

Step 1. Practice the conversation with a partner.

A: Good morning. Health Clinic.
Can I help you?
B: My name is **Balbir Patel.** I'd like to
make an appointment.
A: All right. Can you come in **Friday at 2:00?**
B: **Friday at 2:00?** Yes, that's fine.
A: How do you spell your name please?
B: **B-A-L-B-I-R P-A-T-E-L.**

Step 2. Change partners. Practice the conversation again. Use other days and times for
appointments.

3 Read and Think

Step 1. Look at the picture. Les Green is talking on the phone and ordering supplies.

Step 2. Read the text.

Les Green is busy on the phone today. Many
people are calling for appointments at the clinic.
Les also calls to order supplies for the clinic.
Today he's ordering office supplies: paper,
pens, paper clips, and envelopes. Les enjoys talking
to people on the phone.

Step 3. Look at the vocabulary on pages 111 and 112. Then read the text again.

Vocabulary

Office Supplies

a notepad

a folder

a computer disk

scissors

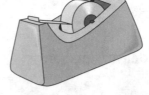

tape

paper clips

Activities

take a message

2 boxes.

order supplies

4:00?

make an appointment

call back

Job Titles

switchboard operator

typist

file clerk

manager

delivery person

security guard

Word Match

A. Listen and match the supplies with the worker.

1.

   a. security guard

2.

   b. file clerk

3.

   c. manager

4.

   d. typist

5.

   e. delivery person

6.

   f. switchboard operator

B. Write the names of the supplies on the correct boxes.

computer disks
paper clips

paper
tape

envelopes
stapler

54233-543

43-9882-J

KX-988500

_____

_____

_____

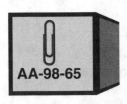
AA-98-65

333-9325L

347996-X

_____

_____

_____

4 Put It in Writing

Look at the appointment slip. Then answer the questions.

> Dr. Kline, M.D.
>
> Southside Health Clinic 22 Hayden Street, Morristown, NJ
>
> _____ John Williams _____
>
> has an appointment
>
> on ___ Wed., July 12 ___ at ___ 9:30 ___ A.M./P.M.
>
> Please call if you cannot keep the appointment.
>
> 484-2222

1. Who has an appointment? ___ John Williams. _____

2. What time is his appointment? _____

3. What day is the appointment? _____

4. Is it in the morning or in the afternoon? _____

5. Where is the clinic? _____

6. What's the phone number of the clinic? _____

5 Listen and Speak

Step 1. Listen to the conversation.

> A: Hello. Can I speak to **Arnold Novak,** please?
> B: Just a minute. I'm sorry. He's busy right now. Can I take a message?
> A: Yes. This is **Isabel Morales.** I received a message from **Mr. Novak** yesterday, and I'm returning his call. I was **at work,** and he called me at home.
> B: OK. Can I have your number, please?
> A: Sure. It's **822-9314.** Thank you.

Step 2. Practice the conversation with a partner.

Step 3. Change partners. Practice again using your own name and phone number.

6 Read and Write

Step 1. Read the information on the order form and fill in the missing amounts.

Purchase Order # 81290				
Date	7/24			
Code	**Item**	**Quantity**	**Unit Price**	**Amount**
F3348	Scissors	1	5.99	
R2117	Glue	1 box	3.75	
S9962	Envelopes	3 boxes	0.85	
S1004	Paper	2 cases	5.50	
S3631	Notepads	1 case	7.80	
			TOTAL	

Step 2. Write the answers to the questions.

1. What is the code for glue? _____*R2117*_____

2. How many boxes of envelopes are they ordering? _____

3. How much is one case of paper? _____

4. How much are two cases of paper? _____

5. What is S3631? _____

6. What is the total of the order? _____

Step 3. With a partner, compare your answers.

Form and Function

1 Can I speak to Mr. Novak, please?

Can	I, you, he, she, it, we, they	speak . . . ?

Examples

Can you **order** some paper? Sure.
Can I **talk** with Ms. Jones? No, you **can't** right now.

Can you **type?** Yes, I **can.**
Can you **use** a computer? Yes, I **can.**

Practice 1

A. **Listen. Circle "?" if you hear a question. Circle "." if you hear a statement.**

1. (?) .   2. ? .   3. ? .   4. ? .

B. **Write a request with *can* for each sentence. Use the words below.**

order   call back later   help me

1. We need some more pencils. _____

2. I'm sorry. I can't talk now. _____

3. This box is really heavy. _____

C. **With a partner, practice each of the requests above.**

2 I'm going to be busy all day Friday.

I'm (I am)	**going to** be busy.	**Are**	we, you, they	**going to** be busy?
You're (you **are**)		**Am**	I	
He's (he **is**)		**Is**	he, she, it	
It's (it **is**)				
We're (we **are**)		**What**	**are** we, you, they	**going to** do?
They're (they **are**)			**am** I	
			is he, she, it	

Examples

First, **I'm going to** call the people on this list. Then **I'm going to** call the people on the other list.
But **I'm not going to** work past 5:00 today.
A: **What are you going to** do tomorrow? B: **I'm going to** see a movie.

Practice 2

A. Listen. Circle the words you hear.

1. going   (going to)   **3.** going   going to   **5.** going   going to

2. going   going to   **4.** going   going to   **6.** going   going to

B. When are you going to do the things below? Write sentences with *going to*.

Example: *I'm going to leave class at 4:00 today.*

1. (leave class) _____

2. (go home) _____

3. (do your homework) _____

4. (go to the store) _____

C. Look at a partner's sentences. When is he or she going to do the things above? Write sentences about your partner on a separate sheet of paper.

D. What are you going to do tomorrow? Tell a partner. Then tell the class about your partner.

3 Mr. Novak called yesterday.

I You He She We They	call**ed**.	I You He She We They	**did not call.** **(didn't)**	**Did**	I you he she we they	**call?**

Examples

They **cleaned** the rooms on the first floor.
Did you **call** the clinic?
What did she **order**?

Did we **finish** all the work? No, we **didn't finish** it yet.
Yes, I **called** yesterday.
She **ordered** two boxes of envelopes.

Practice 3

A. Listen. Circle the words you hear. 🔲

1. help   (helped)
2. answer   answered
3. fix   fixed

4. count   counted
5. wash   washed
6. arrive   arrived

B. Fill in the correct form of the verbs in the sentences.

1. Anton isn't at home. He didn't _____*finish*_____ (finish) work yet.

2. They _____ (start) at 8:00 yesterday.

3. Last Saturday I _____ (clean) the kitchen.

4. They _____ (work) in a factory from 1992 to 1994.

5. When _____ you _____ (order) the paper?

6. We _____ (call) you last night.

7. You didn't _____ (watch) TV last night.

8. We _____ (cook) dinner at 7:00.

C. Work with a partner. Ask questions with *did*.

Example: A: Did Anton call the clinic yesterday? B: No, he didn't.

Student A: Find out what Anton did yesterday. Circle the answers.

wash the windows	call the clinic	study English	play soccer
listen to the radio	walk to the park	mail some letters	
visit some friends	fix the car	work all day	

Now answer your partner's questions about Isabel.

Yesterday Isabel worked all day. After work, she mailed some letters and walked to the park. She also called the clinic. Finally, she washed the windows.

Student B: Answer your partner's questions about what Anton did yesterday.

Yesterday Anton visited some friends and played soccer. They listened to the radio and studied English for a while. Anton also fixed his car.

Ask questions to find out what Isabel did. Circle the answers.

wash the windows	call the clinic	study English	play soccer
listen to the radio	walk to the park	mail some letters	
visit some friends	fix the car	work all day	

Now compare your answers.

D. Tell a friend what you did yesterday. Then tell a friend what you did last Saturday.

E. Write about your friend's activities below.

_____

_____

_____

_____

_____

_____

Putting It to Work

1 Pair Work

Step 1. Listen. Fill in the missing information on the order form.

Purchase Order No. 81290				
To Southside Health Clinic 22 Hayden St.				
Code	**Item**	**Quantity**	**Unit Price**	**Amount**
	Scissors		5.99	
R2117		1 box		
S9962	Envelopes	boxes		
		cases	5.50	
	Notepads	1 case		
			TOTAL _____	

Step 2. With a partner, compare your answers.

2 Pair Work

Step 1. Listen to the conversation.

> A: Can you **go to the library** with me on **Thursday?**
> B: Yes, I can. What time?
> A: Is **4:30** OK?
> B: That's fine.

Step 2. Make some appointments with your partner.

Student A: Make the appointments below with your partner:

Sun.	Mon.	Tues.	Wed.	Thurs.	Fri.	Sat.
						Study: 8:00 A.M.
Store 3:00	Movie: 8:00			Library: 4:30		

Now your partner will make some appointments with you. Write them on the correct days.

Student B: Your partner will make some appointments with you. Write them in the schedule below.

Then make the appointments below with your partner.

Sun.	Mon.	Tues.	Wed.	Thurs.	Fri.	Sat.
		Doctor: 9:00				
			Class: 7:30		Soccer: 2:00	Party: 8:00 P.M.

Step 3. Now compare your schedules.

3 Group/Class Work

Step 1. What supplies do they use at work? Write the supplies.

Typist   Housekeeper   Receptionist

_____   _____   _____

_____   _____   _____

_____   _____   _____

_____   _____   _____

_____   _____   _____

_____   _____   _____

Step 2. Compare your answers with the others in the class.

4 Culture Work

You are the receptionist. What can you say? What can you do?

Picture Dictionary

The Body

ear   eye   head   neck   back   arm   hand   leg   knee   foot

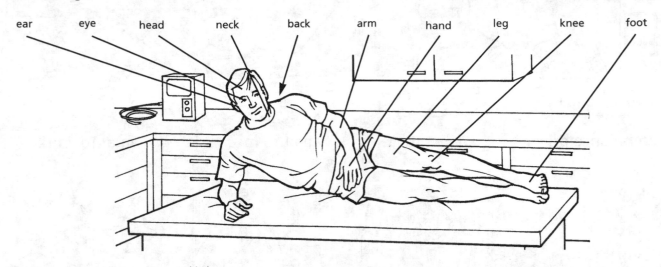

The House

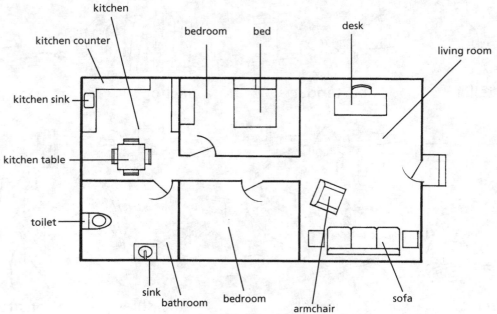

kitchen
kitchen counter
kitchen sink
kitchen table
toilet
sink
bathroom
bedroom
bed
desk
living room
bedroom
armchair
sofa

Groceries

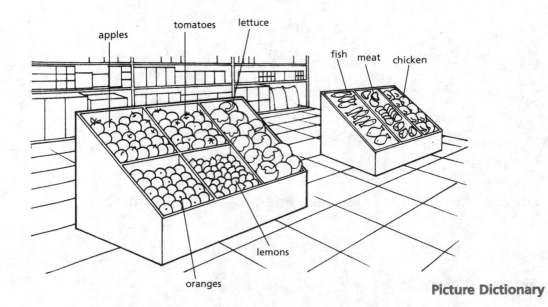

apples
tomatoes
lettuce
fish   meat   chicken
lemons
oranges

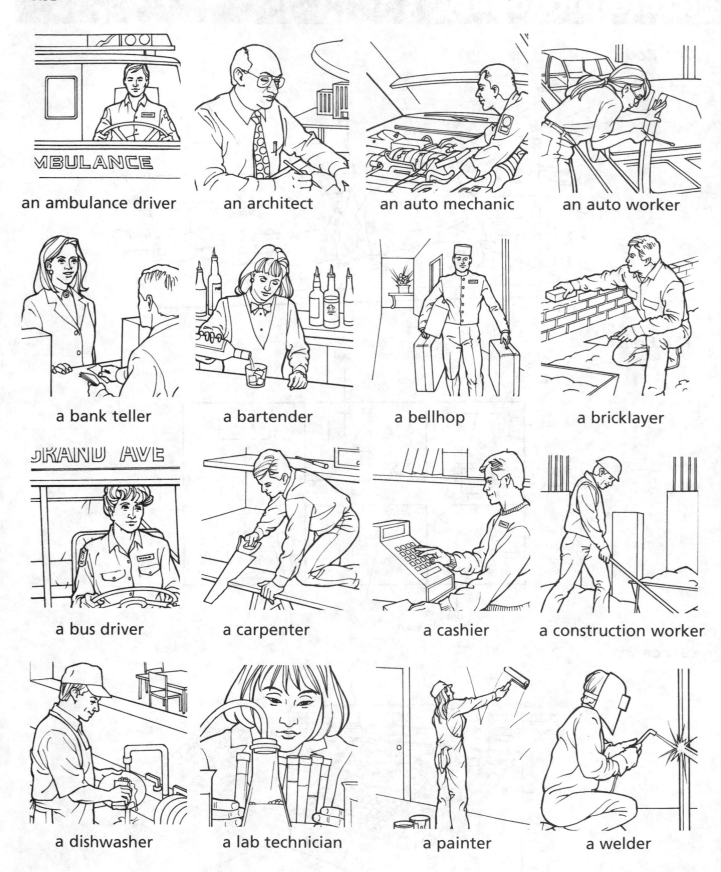

an ambulance driver · an architect · an auto mechanic · an auto worker

a bank teller · a bartender · a bellhop · a bricklayer

a bus driver · a carpenter · a cashier · a construction worker

a dishwasher · a lab technician · a painter · a welder